Property of Don Busath

Property of Don Busath

MAHONRI
YOUNG
HIS LIFE AND ART

MAHONRI YOUNG

YOUNG

HIS LIFE AND ART

THOMAS E. TOONE

Signature Books

Salt Lake City

For my children

David, Kristine, Jonathan, Matthew,

Daniel, Mark, Luke

JACKET DESIGN BY RON STUCKI

∞ *Mahonri Young: His Life and Art* was printed on acid-free paper and was composed, printed, and bound in the United States.

2000   99   98   97   6   5   4   3   2   1

Library of Congress Cataloging-in-Publication Data
Toone, Thomas Ernest.
Mahonri Young : his life and art / by Thomas E. Toone
p.   cm.
Includes bibliographical references.
ISBN 1-56085-055-8
1. Young, Mahonri Mackintosh, 1877-1957
2. Sculptors—United States—Biography.   I. Title.
NB237.Y68T66   1966
730'.92—dc20
[B]   96-21198
CIP

Contents

Preface

This book has been a long time in the making. It began as my dissertation at Pennsylvania State University. I wish to acknowledge those whom I worked with there, including professors George Mauner, Roland Fleischer, Brent Wilson, and especially Jeanne Chenualt Porter, for her support and friendship through the years.

Special thanks to William Smart, for his careful reading of the manuscript. His insights and editorial suggestions proved invaluable. I want to acknowledge Dr. Eugene Fairbanks, son of sculptor Avard Fairbanks, for allowing me to publish his recollections of the This is the Place Monument commission and the drawing of his father's design. Norma Davis also read part of the manuscript and gave helpful suggestions.

Collecting photographs of Mahonri Young's work was an imposing task. I want to acknowledge various institutions and museums and their staffs, especially the Metropolitan Museum of Art, the Whitney Museum of American Art, and the American Museum of Natural History. Thanks to the Museum of Art and its staff at Brigham Young University for their time and assistance, especially Julia Lippert and David Hawkinson. Thanks also to Manuscripts and

Special Collections at BYU's Harold B. Lee Library for their help, especially Tom Wells and Sue Thompson. I want to thank the staff at the LDS church's Museum of Church History and Art, Robert Davis, and especially R. T. Clark whose assistance and encouragement were greatly appreciated. At Utah State University the Nora Eccles Harrison Museum of Art and the College of History, Arts, and Social Sciences were also helpful and supportive. Special thanks to Craig Law for his photographic work, as well as his knowledge of the medium and help in choosing illustrations for this book. His friendship and help are greatly appreciated. I owe a debt of gratitude to those writers I have consulted.

Through the years my family has been crucial in sustaining my effort and I appreciate their support. To parents on both sides, Clarella Toone and Dr. Thomas and Beverly Smart, and to my wife and children go my deep-felt thanks and gratitude. The words always seem trite until you have gone through the experience of writing a book. Hopefully, my children, whose constant "How's the book going, Dad" meant a lot, will now get their dad back. And Dotti, with her unfailing support and encouragement, made it all possible.

Chronology

1877   Mahonri Mackintosh Young was born August 9 to Mahonri Moriancumer Young and Agnes Mackintosh in Salt Lake City, Utah Territory. His first home was the Deseret Woolen Mills (the factory) until age seven.

1884   Death of his father, Mahonri Moriancumer Young. The family sells the factory and moves to Salt Lake City and a house at 174 C Street.

1885   Starts school, first at a home school and then at the Twentieth Ward School. His close boyhood friends include many who would later become artists, John Held, Jr., Lee Greene Richards, Jack Sears, and Alma Wright.

1890   Does first sculpture—a small wooden relief of Julius Caesar.

1894   At age seventeen, he quits school after one day of high school. Starts working to earn money to study art with James T. Harwood, John Hafen, and Edwin Evans. Young's fellow students include Alma Wright, Lee Greene Richards, and Earl Cummings. First artist job with *Salt Lake Herald*, and then *The Salt Lake Tribune* where he worked for almost four years as a sketch artist and portrait engraver.

1899   Studies at the Art Students League in New York City for eight months. There his teachers include George B. Bridgeman, Kenyon Cox, and Robert Blum. Also attends lectures by George de Forest Brush, Bryson Burroughs, and John H. Twachtman.

1900   After his return to Salt Lake City, he works as the head photo engraver for the *Salt Lake Herald*.

1901   By the end of the year he has enough money to go to Paris. Enrolls at the Académie Julian and studies with Jean-Paul Laurens. Rooms with Howard McCormick whom he met at the Art Students League.

1902   Meets George Luks and becomes friends with Alfred Maurer. Makes a three-week trip to Italy with fellow students and visits Venice, Florence, Milan, Padua, and Rome. After his return to Paris he decides to take up sculpture.

1903   Studies sculpture at the Académie Julian with Charles Raoul Verlet, and later with Jean-Antoine Injalbert at the Académie Colarossi. Attends drawing classes at the Académie Delecluse. Sculpts first important laborers, *The Shoveler* and *Man Tired*. Returns home to Salt Lake City in the summer and back to Paris in the fall to study for two more years.

1904   Works increasingly on his own. Sculpts *Bovet-Arthur—A Laborer*, *Alfy*, *Stevedore*, and *The Chiseler*.

1905   As his years in Paris come to a close, he makes a three-month visit to Italy before he returns to Salt Lake City. On his trip home he meets Robert Henri in New York.

1906   Teaches art classes at the YMCA in Salt Lake where John Held, Jr., is his student. Sculpts portrait busts of Cecelia Sharp and B. H. Roberts.

1907   Marries Cecelia Sharp on February 9. Commissioned to do Joseph and Hyrum Smith statues. Does portrait bust of Alfred Lambourne. Proposes Sea Gull Monument to LDS church.

1908   Birth of daughter Agnes Young.

1909   Deseret Gym frieze.

1910   Moves to New York City. Begins sculpting small bronzes of common man and returns to the theme of labor.

1911   Starts commission for the sculpture reliefs and figures for the Technical High School (West High School) building in Salt Lake City, Utah. *Bovet-Arthur—A Laborer* wins the Helen Foster Barnett Prize for sculpture. Sculpts *Man with a Heavy Sledge*. A son, Mahonri Sharp Young, is born on July 23.

1912 Becomes a member of the Association of American Painters and Sculptors, organizers of the Armory Show. Receives the commission for the Hopi Habitat Group for the American Museum of Natural History in New York City. Makes his first trip to Arizona. Howard McCormick paints the scenery for the commission, Young sculpts the figures. Receives commission for the Sea Gull Monument. Elected to the National Academy of Design as an associate member.

1913 Exhibits at Armory Show. Dedication of the Sea Gull Monument at Salt Lake City, Utah, on October 1.

1914 Moves to Leonia, New Jersey. Panama-Pacific International Exposition commission for sculptures of laborers for the Liberal Arts and Manufacturers Palace.

1915 Receives second commission from the American Museum of Natural History for the Apache Habitat Group. Makes a trip to Arizona to do studies for the commission with John Held, Jr. Visits Panama-Pacific International Exposition in San Francisco, where he receives a Silver Medal for Sculpture.

1916 Completes the Apache Habitat Group for the American Museum of Natural History. Sculpts *The Rigger*. Begins teaching at the Art Students League.

1917 Receives final commission from the American Museum of Natural History for the Navajo Habitat Group. Makes a trip to Arizona to do preliminary studies. His wife, Cecelia Sharp Young, dies at Leonia, New Jersey.

1918 Major exhibit of his work at the Sculptor's Gallery in New York City.

1923 Monument to the Dead for the American Cathedral of the Holy Trinity (American Pro-Cathedral) in Paris, France. Made a full member of the National Academy of Design.

1924 Unveiling of the Navajo Habitat Group.

1925 Eldridge Adams becomes Young's patron, enabling the artist to move with his children to Paris for two and a half years.

1926 Starts sculpture for Pioneer Woman Memorial competition. Begins prizefighter sculptures with *Right to the Jaw* and *On the Button*.

1927 Young loses the Pioneer Woman Memorial competition. Continues to sculpt prize-fighters: *The Knockdown* and *Da Winnah*.

1928   Returns to New York City. First exhibition of his prizefighters at the Rehn
        Gallery in New York. Begins commission from Phoenix Hosiery Company.

1929   Article for the *Encyclopedia Britannica* on the theory of modeling. Works in
        Hollywood, California, for 20th Century Fox Studio. Does portrait-relief
        medallians for the new 20th Century Fox Music Building and the Fox Studio
        Laboratory of Technical Research, life-size sculpture of the prizefighter Joe
        Gans, and busts for the Paul Muni film *Seven Faces*. Completes commission
        from Phoenix Hosiery Company.

1931   Marries Dorothy Weir, daughter of the American impressionist painter J.
        Alden Weir, February 17. The couple honeymoons in France and Spain.

1932   *The Knockdown* wins a gold medal for sculpture at the Los Angeles Olympic
        Games Exhibition. Moves to Weir farm at Brachville, Connecticut, and sets
        up studio there.

1934   The etching *Pont Neuf* included in "Fine Prints of the Year, 1933." Begins
        teaching again, instructor of sculpture at the Art Students League.

1935   Retrospective show of his etching at the Kraushaar Galleries in New York.
        Attends the unveiling of the Father Kino Memorial in Tucson, Arizona.
        Extended visit to Salt Lake City where he does preliminary work for his
        design of the This is the Place Monument. Elected to the National Institute
        of Arts and Letters.

1936   Dedication of the Father Kino Memorial at Tucson, Arizona. Spends most of
        the summer in Salt Lake City campaigning for the This is the Place Monument
        Commission.

1938   Receives commission for old Salt Lake Theatre Memorial Plaque.

1939   Monumental figures of *Industry* and *Agriculture* for the 1939 New York World's
        Fair. Wins commission for the This is the Place Monument.

1940   Addison Gallery of American Art holds major retrospective show, Phillips
        Academy, Andover, Massachusetts.

1941   Final contract for the This is the Place Monument.

1945   Receives commission for *Brigham Young* statue for U.S. Capitol Rotunda.

1946   Goes to Rome to work on *Brigham Young* statue.

1947   Young's wife, Dorothy Weir Young, dies of cancer on May 28. Dedication of the
            This is the Place Monument on July 24. Elected a member of the American
            Academy of Arts, Music, and Literature.

1948-49   Completes *Brigham Young* statue in Rome.

1950   June 1, *Brigham Young* statue unveiled at the National Statuary Hall, U.S. Capitol
            Rotunda, Washington, D.C. Young makes his last trip to Utah where he is made
            an honorary lifetime member of the Sons of Utah Pioneers club.

1955   Participates in the Armory Show Commemorative Exhibition in New York
            City, June 1.

1957   At age eighty, Mahonri Young dies at Norwalk, Connecticut, on November 2.

Spanish Explorers: Fathers Escalante and Dominguez Group, 1946-47

BRONZE, MONUMENTAL
(This is the Place Monument,
This is the Place State Park,
Salt Lake City, Utah.
Photo by Craig Law)

CHAPTER ONE.

The Greatest Day of My Life

*The challenge to everyman's conscience is to choose for his life's work
the thing he loves to do, and once he has decided upon a course, he must work conscientiously
to learn all about it. There is in the heart of an ambitious, sincere man—to do well—
that which in his honest opinion he knows to be right.*

—Mahonri Young

After eighty-nine days on the trail they made camp on the Bear River near the Utah-Wyoming border. Since leaving Fort Bridger, members of the company had been struck with a mysterious illness they called Mountain Fever. Brigham Young was so sick that he could not travel any farther. A council was held and it was decided to send a party of twenty-three wagons and forty-two men on ahead to find and clear the trail.

That first company of Mormon pioneers had left Winter Quarters, Nebraska, in mid-April 1847. Their journey was an act of faith, for, although they had read about the land, not one of them had seen their final destination. Basing decisions on maps of earlier explorers and descriptions of the region by trappers and traders, they headed to the Great Basin on the west side of the Rocky Mountains, the valley of the Great Salt Lake, a place not yet well known and still unsettled by anglos. That was what made the region attractive. By settling there

they would be free from the indignity they had suffered in Missouri and Illinois at the hands of intolerant neighbors. This company of 148 souls and seventy-three wagons would be the first of thousands to pour into the Great Basin.

On 14 July Orson Pratt led an advance company to find the trail left by the Donner Party the year before. This would be the most difficult part of the journey. The going was slow, the trail so overgrown it was difficult to find. In places they inched along, clearing the trail with axe, pick, and shovel. The canyon was so steep that wagon wheels had to be double-locked to keep them from plummeting to obliteration. Slowly they moved up and over Little Mountain, then down Emigration Canyon.

On 21 July scouts from the advance party caught the first glimpse of the valley of the Great Salt Lake. The next day they rode in, followed by the main wagon train on 23 July. Brigham Young, still weak from Mountain Fever, arrived at an over-look a little after noon on 24 July. As the last wag-ons emerged from the canyon, Young's carriage was brought to a halt. According to later reminiscences he lifted himself on one elbow to survey the vast valley and pronounced, "This is the right place. Drive on." That date and those words have become legendary in Utah history.

One hundred years later, on 24 July 1947, thou-sands of people gathered at that place on a hill, then called Pioneer View, to attend the dedication of the This is the Place Monument. The day was hot and clear and hundreds of sea gulls circled gracefully overhead. The dedication stand was filled with dignitaries. Among them, Mahonri Young, sculptor of the large monument and grand-son of Brigham Young, took particular note of the gulls for it was uncommon to see them this far east of the Great Salt Lake. Thinking this was extraordi-nary, he wrote, "All this time the gulls continued to circle in intricate, swinging circles around the monument, some high up in the air, others just over the heads of the people. It was a sublime spec-tacle."[1] To the artist it was a good omen, one which validated his extraordinary accomplishment.

The sculptor soon found, however, that he had not been included on the program and that neither his assistant, Spero Anargyros, nor the monument's architect were to be seated with him on the stand. He spoke to George Albert Smith, president of the Church of Jesus Christ of Latter-day Saints (LDS or Mormon), who was in charge of the dedication program. Smith agreed that Young's colleagues should be invited to the stand and that Young could say a few words.

"Make it short, Hon," Smith said, referring to him by his nickname.

"Five minutes?" Mahonri replied.

"No, shorter."

"All right, one."

When it came his turn, Young rose and said: "My friends, in two weeks, come the ninth of Au-gust, I will be seventy years old. This is the great-est day of my life. I thank you." He then sat down.[2]

For Young this day marked the crowning achievement of his career. It was a day he had long envisioned, for he had fought hard to win this commission and spent years bringing it to completion. The monument was the largest, most time-consuming and personally important commis-sion he ever undertook. He always referred to it as "The Big Job."

Given its massive size and scope, the This is the Place Monument would be considered the cap-stone to any sculptor's career. Its granite base was eighty-six feet long. The monument rose sixty feet into the sky, with three main sculptural groups, the tallest of which stood eighteen feet. Reliefs cov-ered major portions of the flat surfaces of the base. In all, it included over 144 large scale images, of which seventy-four were human figures. It cost close to one-half million dollars.

The work was important to Young for personal reasons, for it was about his heritage. Years earlier in a letter to a life-long friend, Young wrote: "All my life I have been interested in the western migra-tion of our people. It always seems to me to be one of the greatest epics of the world. I have dreamed and hoped that some day Utah could find the will and means to let me make a monument to the pio-neers, adequate to their great achievements. I would be willing to spend years of my life on it and make it my crowning masterpiece."[3]

By the time Young won the This is the Place Monument commission, he had already established himself as an internationally prominent sculptor.

Mahonri Young and his assistant Spero Anargyros
with two of the central figures for the This is the Place Monument
(Photographic Archives, Harold B. Lee Library,
Brigham Young University, Provo, Utah)

His small bronzes of laborers and prize fighters had brought him critical and popular acclaim on two continents. Young's work had found its way into the collections of major American museums, and he had done significant commissioned representations from Paris to Hollywood. He was a member of the National Academy, National Academy of Design, Institute of Arts and Letters, Society of American Etchers, American Academy of Arts and Letters, and the Century and National Arts clubs. Among his many awards and prizes were the Helen Foster Barnett Prize for sculpture from the National Academy of Design in 1911, a silver medal from the Panama-Pacific International Exposition in 1915, first prize for sculpture at the 1932 Olympic exhibition in Los Angeles, and many national awards for his prints.[4]

As his professional achievements indicate, Young was versatile. He was not only a sculptor but a painter and printmaker, and his fellow artists recognized in him a superb draftsman. He drew incessantly. His suits were tailored with extra-large pockets to accommodate a sketchbook. In a tribute to Young, fellow artist Harry Wickey said: "From the beginning of his career Mahonri Young decided that whatever else he might become, he would take special care not to become a specialist. Keeping his word, he has made hundreds of drawings [and large] numbers of watercolors, paintings, etchings and sculpture of the most varied subject matter. These include animals, laborers, prize fighters, portraits, and landscapes. In fact, it would almost seem that everything Young saw found graphic expression in one medium or another."[5] Those who knew Young said that art was his life, that he was always working or talking about art.

This versatility was also apparent in his teaching. Young taught at the Art Students League in New York City between 1916 and 1943. According to Steward Klonis, the league's director, Young was the only instructor to teach in three different media, besides being one of the first to offer a class in printmaking.[6] By the time he retired, he had taught everything in the curriculum. Students often asked this popular instructor, "Which do you prefer, Mr. Young, painting or sculpture?" to which he responded:

Now I have been asked this question so many times that, just in the natural course of events, an answer has evolved itself. It generally goes something like this. You see, when I am modeling in the round, I'm sure there's nobody more skillful or who knows more about relief, high or low, than myself: but when I turn to relief, high or low, I realize that the thing I've worked at and thought most about is drawing: that, of course, I know is the basic Art: but upon taking a piece of paper and a crayon or charcoal I find it has its difficulties, it is messy and lacks definition, so I turn to one of my earliest loves— pen and ink—that, at least, does what you want: but, lo and behold, the paper does not take the ink readily—it's greasy—the pen sputters, scratches, fails to flow and blubs, making ink spots, large and small, over the paper, so I put some watercolor on it, or pastel, and it looks a bit better. I feel that, perhaps, water color is what I can do and so I make my start in ink or pencil and go on in watercolor. I try to heighten the lights with gouache but it doesn't work well; it dries out lighter—goes soft and mushy or it is too sharp and brittle so I pick up pastel; and then realize that I ought to be working in oil if I'm going to carry out what I'm trying to do, into full color and tone; but that too has more difficulties than almost any of the other mediums and anyway, there's a perfectly good relief in the group of figures I'm doing or perhaps that figure would make a fine statuette in the round; and there you see I've made the circle and I am back to where I started, set to do it all over again. I sometimes

THE ARTIST IN HIS STUDIO, CA. 1922
(PHOTOGRAPHIC ARCHIVES, HAROLD B. LEE LIBRARY,
BRIGHAM YOUNG UNIVERSITY, PROVO, UTAH)

think of myself as a squirrel in a cage or a kitten chasing his tail. I like the kitten simile better; it is pleasanter and I feel more truthful. In consequence of all this I'm never bored; I only lose interest when I'm tired, otherwise Art is a continual delight, trouble and irritation.[7]

Young executed a vast amount of work. At his death his estate alone included 320 pieces of sculpture, 590 oil paintings, 5,500 watercolors, 2,600 prints, and thousands of drawings. Although he worked extensively in other media, it was sculpture that brought him his first recognition and success as well as his largest and most important commissions. Sculpture was the heart of his career. In 1940 Young had a major retrospective show of his work, and for the catalogue he was asked to write

an autobiographical sketch. He titled it "Notes at the Beginnings" and opened with the statement, "I cannot remember when I did not want to be a sculptor."[8]

There are two important primary sources for information on Young's life. The first is the artist's own writings. Through most of his life he kept a journal and saved much of his correspondence. During his later years, when his health began to fail and he was unable to work as much as he would have liked, he turned to writing his life history with the intention of publishing it. Although he never completed this project, he left voluminous handwritten notes. The second source is Jack Sears, a life-long friend and fellow artist. Sears, who planned to write a book on Young, collected and saved all the information he could. These two sources provide a wealth of information on the artist and the period of history through which he lived.

Mahonri was born on 9 August 1877 in Salt Lake City. For his first eight years his home was the Deseret Woolen Mills, but with his father's death, the family moved into town. It was here, during his teenage years, that Young received his first art training under James T. Harwood, a Utah artist who had studied in Paris and exhibited there. Young soon put his talents to use working for several Salt Lake City newspapers as a sketch artist, all the while saving his money so he could continue his studies in the East. In 1899 he set out for the Art Students League in New York City. There he took classes from such prominent artists as Kenyon Cox, George B. Bridgeman, and John H. Twachtman. In 1901 he went to Paris to study at the Académie Julian, where a whole new world of art and museums opened to him. Paris was the center of the art world, and all around him lived the artists who would be most influential in pointing the direction art would take for the next fifty years. During those years Young developed many close associations and life-long friends, including Leo Stein and Alfred Maurer, both of whom were closely associated with the beginnings of the modern art movement in Europe and America. It was here that Young did his first bronzes of laborers, *The Shoveler* and *Man Tired*, which brought him recognition and his first critical acclaim.

He returned to Utah in 1905 hoping to establish himself as a sculptor. For the next five years he worked hard, doing several portrait busts of prominent people in Salt Lake City, the *Joseph Smith* and *Hyrum Smith* statues for the LDS church, and a few smaller commissions. Through this period he felt a great deal of frustration because commissions were so hard to come by and there was never enough work for an artist to make ends meet. He felt that the population at large did not value or understand art. Because of this he decided that if he really wanted a career he would have to move to New York City, which he did in 1910. His struggles to establish himself continued, but slowly things began to break. In 1911 *Bovet-Arthur—A Laborer* won a prestigious national award for sculpture. The next year he received a commission from the LDS church to do the Sea Gull Monument. During this time he was an active member of the Association of American Painters and Sculptors, and in 1913 he helped organize and participated in the famous Armory Show. He received a major commission from the American Museum of Natural History in New York City, as well. The figures he sculpted for their southwest Indian exhibit were so well received that the commission gave him more work and kept him busy and financially secure well into the next decade.

The 1920s was a busy and productive time. He made two trips to Paris, the first in 1923 to sculpt Monument to the Dead for the American Cathedral of the Holy Trinity; the second in 1926 extended into a stay of two and one-half years. This was when Young did most of the bronzes of prize fighters which brought him the greatest success and recognition of his career. In 1941 *Life* magazine referred to Young as "the George Bellows of American sculpture."[9] His years in Paris were among the best of his life. In this, his favorite city, he renewed old acquaintances and worked freely and productively.

The decade ended with Young in Hollywood, California, for three months, working for 20th Century Fox Film Studio. During the 1930s and 1940s

Young's work turned increasingly to western themes. There were small bronzes and major commissions, the largest and most important of which was the This is the Place Monument, which occupied most of the last productive years of his career. With its completion there was still one more work that he wanted to do as long as his health held out: the *Brigham Young* statue for the National Statuary Hall at the U.S. Capitol. It seemed fitting that his last major commission was a tribute to his famous grandfather. After its dedication in 1951, the artist's health grew steadily worse, and on 2 November 1957 he died at Norwalk, Connecticut. The next day the headline of a *New York Times* article read, "Mahonri Young, Sculptor, Dead. Grandson of Mormon Leader Was Noted For Bronzes—Taught Students Here."[10]

Young's professional reputation was two-fold. He appeared at a time of transition in American art. Although he never was influenced by the modern art movement, his works played a key role in the development of modern sculpture. Throughout the last half of the nineteenth century sculpture was dominated by monuments, official portraits, and architectural decoration, and tended to be conservative and dictated by public taste. It was Young and others who, at the beginning of the twentieth century, brought sculpture off its pedestal and transformed it into a free and independent means of expression. In relationship to this Daniel Robbins has noted that "the principal accomplishment of the main line of early twentieth-century modern sculpture was to win for the medium the right to be . . . as independent as easel painting."[11]

Young's work, especially his small bronzes of laborers and prize fighters, played a significant role in that push for independence and free form, and this alone has assured him a significant place in the history of American sculpture. But there is more. In the West, and especially in Utah, he was recognized for his grand depictions of frontier heroism. Heir to a pioneer legacy and grandson of the colonizer of Utah, he left a sculptural testament to the themes he had honored throughout his life—his Mormon roots, Native American culture, and the independence of frontiersmen and explorers, all of whom were a part of the history and lore of the great American West. This, combined with his expressive and realistic small bronzes, assured his national reputation and established for him a permanent place in the history of twentieth-century art.

Notes

1. Mahonri M. Young, "This is the Place Monument," Mahonri Young Collection, Mss. 4, box 7, folder 17, Archives and Manuscripts, Harold B. Lee Library, Brigham Young University, Provo, Utah.

2. Ibid.

3. Mahonri Young to Jack Sears, Jack Sears Collection, Mss. 1058, box 3, Archives and Manuscripts, Lee Library.

4. For a complete list of Young's awards, honors, affiliations, and exhibitions to the year 1934, see "Mahonri Mackintosh Young—Sculptor and Engraver," *Index of Twentieth-Century Artists* (New York: Research Institute of the College Art Association, 1933-37), 2:45-48.

5. Quoted in Shirley Kazuko Yonemori, "Mahonri Mackintosh Young, Printmaker," M.A. thesis, Brigham Young University, 1963, 116.

6. Author's interview with Steward Klonis, Art Students League, New York City, Aug. 1979; *One Hundred Prints by 100 Artists of the Art Students League of New York, 1875-1975* (New York: Art Students League of New York, 1975), 136.

7. Young, "Notes at the Beginning," box 6, folder 42.

8. Young, "Notes at the Beginning," in *Mahonri M. Young: Retrospective Exhibition* (Andover, MA: Addison Gallery of American Art, 1940), 47.

9. "Mahonri Young's Sculpture Preserves His Mormon Past," *Life*, 17 Feb. 1941, 76-78.

10. *New York Times*, 3 Nov. 1957.

11. Tom Armstrong et al., *200 Years of American Sculpture* (New York: Whitney Museum of American Art, 1976), 135.

CHAPTER TWO.

The Factory

The Jesuits say, let us have the child until he is seven years old and you may have him the rest of his life.

—Mahonri Young

Mahonri Mackintosh Young's parents were Agnes Mackintosh (1857-1943) and Mahonri Moriancumer Young (1858-84). Agnes was the only child of Daniel Mackintosh's second wife, Ellen Nightingale. In her later years she came to live with the Youngs at the Deseret Woolen Mills. The family referred to her as Grannie.[1] Mahonri Moriancumer was the only son of Margaret M. Alley and Brigham Young. When Margaret died, Mahonri Moriancumer was taken in by Clara Decker Young, the plural wife whom Brigham brought with him on the vanguard trek across the plains in 1847.[2] At the time of the artist's birth, Utah was still a territory. It had been only thirty years since the first Mormons entered the Salt Lake Valley and eight since the railroad connected the continent at Promontory, Utah. With the railroad came progress and an abrupt end to the pioneer era. Crossing the Great Plains, which had formerly taken months, was now accomplished in days. No longer was Salt Lake City an isolated settlement but a thriving city and a major crossroads of the West.

At the time it was a common practice to name children after famous people. In the case of Mahonri, this unusual name had its origin in Mormon history and scripture. While residing in Kirtland, Ohio, Reynolds Cahoon had a son born to him. One day, while church founder Joseph Smith was passing by his door, Cahoon called to him and asked him to bless and name the baby. Smith did so and gave the name Mahonri Moriancumer. When he finished, Smith laid the child on the bed, turned to the father, and reportedly said: "The name I have given your son is the name of the Brother of Jared; the Lord has just shown it to me." William F. Cahoon, who was standing nearby, heard the Mormon prophet say this and commented that the name of an important, though mysterious, Book of Mormon figure had just been revealed.[3]

When it came time to name their child, Mahonri's mother Agnes wanted her son to bear

9

ABOVE:
MAHONRI MORIANCUMER YOUNG
FROM WILLIAM CLAWSON'S PAINTING

OPPOSITE ABOVE:
AGNES MACKINTOSH

OPPOSITE BELOW:
MAHONRI MACKINTOSH YOUNG

(PHOTOGRAPHIC ARCHIVES,
HAROLD B. LEE LIBRARY,
BRIGHAM YOUNG UNIVERSITY,
PROVO, UTAH)

his father's name, Mahonri Moriancumer, but her husband objected. Even though Mahonri senior had grown up in Salt Lake City when it was still an isolated Mormon settlement, he had endured constant teasing. Now that Utah was no longer secluded, he argued that the odd name would cause his son even more embarrassment. The surname alone had caused him trouble as a youth.[4] In a letter from Mahonri Moriancumer to his father, Brigham Young, the former complained that when he took his horse and buggy to town he would never get any respect because he was "one of the president's boys."[5] It was hard enough being a Young, he insisted, without further attention being called to it by such a peculiar name.

Both parents adamantly held to their point of view, but a compromise was reached. They named the child Mahonri Mackintosh Young, a combination of his father's and mother's names. From childhood on, parents and friends just called him "Hon," but, as his father predicted, it still caused considerable inconvenience and became the source of more than one sandlot fight, as the artist later wrote.[6]

Nevertheless, as he grew older, Mahonri's name became a distinctive signature. At the start of his career he signed his work "M. M. Young." Realizing that his unique first name might be an asset, he changed to "Mahonri Young." By 1917 he signed his work, "Mahonri Y." Later, when his son, Mahonri Sharp Young, a writer, began to publish, the artist signed his work "Mahonri M. Young" or "Mahonri M. Y." Finally he simply signed his name "Mahonri." In a newspaper interview he said, "Do you know Michelangelo's last name or Raphael's or Rembrandt's?"[7]

According to family tradition, Mahonri junior was the last grandchild born while Brigham Young, the famous Mormon leader, was still alive. When the aging patriarch asked about the new addition to the family, the child's parents brought him to the Beehive House in downtown Salt Lake City to receive a blessing. For many years the artist never knew of this meeting. When asked if he had met his grandfather, he would, of course, say no. But there came a day when all that changed:

It all came about in this wise. My very old and very good friends, Jack and Florence Sears, were calling on my mother and during the conversation she told how, when I was old enough for the journey and she was strong enough, she dressed me in my very best bib and tucker and, with my father, took me to call on my Grandfather, who was sick and in bed, but he had strength and desire enough to see me. During the interview he gave me a blessing and put his hand on my head and called me by name. This my mother told to my dear friends Jack and Florence Sears, but never thought to tell me. I like to think of myself dressed as new ones were always dressed in those far away days in white dresses which not only came to their feet but to their mother's feet when she stood up, and underneath, enwrapped with a bellyband, yards in length, of red flannel. I like to think I made an impression upon my Grandfather, but that can be hardly expected as he had so many grandchildren before my arrival. They were no novelty to him. But I think I am honestly going to believe that I was the last one to meet him personally and receive his blessing.

Ever since the knowledge of my early good fortune came to me I have answered the question stated above in the affirmative with a very decided "yes." And then, if more curiosity is displayed and a desire for more information is shown, I tell the story, but not as boldly as above. In fact I generally go on to tell of the long conversation I had with him, though I never tell what we talked about. And then I say, when asked how old I was at the time, that I was born on the ninth of August, 1877, and he died the twenty-ninth of August, 1877.[8]

Proud of his connection to his grandfather, Mahonri also felt that his artistic talent came to him through the Young line. In his "Notes at the Beginning," written as an autobiographical sketch for the catalog of his 1940 retrospective show, he stated:

> If you look back to Pioneer days you will find my grandfather a skilled painter and joiner and after he got to Utah an encourager of all the arts; a passionate lover of the theater; builder, of what was for many years, the largest [pipe] organ in existence; an encourager of an architecture, which, though traditionally colonial, was individual and characteristic enough to be known as Brighamesque.[9]

Young's first home was the Deseret Woolen Mills, owned and operated by his father. Located southeast of Salt Lake City near the mouth of Parleys Canyon, the mill was one of many industries started by President Brigham Young to make the Latter-day Saints as economically independent as possible. As early as 1849 Brigham initiated plans to establish the wool industry. He wrote to church leaders in England concerning the possibility of finding sheep and equipment as well as members knowledgeable and experienced in manufacturing wool. But more pressing concerns, as well as the difficulty of transporting machinery, delayed the arrival of equipment until 1862. The next year "Brigham Young's Woolen and Cotton Factory" located on "Big Kanyon Creek" began operating with 240 spindles, making it the first substantial woolen mill in the West.[10] Later its name was changed to the Deseret Woolen Mills, but Mahonri and family always referred to it as simply "the factory."

The compound consisted of a complex of several buildings arranged in a self-contained enclosure that included the family home, a carpenter shop, a barn, and the building for cleaning and processing wool. The place had a profound and lasting influence on young Mahonri. During the six and one-half years he lived at the factory, his artistic sensitivity awakened, and many of the themes and subjects that appeared later in his art have their genesis there. He later had strong memories of the workers and machines, the moving pulleys and belts, and the strong smell of soap used to clean wool.[11] As a small child he was particularly fascinated by the carpenter shop with its woodworking tools and marvelled at how they were used to fashion objects. As the boy grew older, he spent hours whittling toy guns. Later he confessed: "I used to think that my whittling these guns was because I wanted to have guns. I'm inclined to think differently now. I think that, though I did want the guns, more fundamentally I was carrying out an instinct to carve and model forms."[12]

The artist's father was an avid sportsman and member of the Salt Lake Yacht Club. He had a reputation as a master with the rod and gun, the appreciation of which he must have passed on to his son. As an adult, Hon's father first worked at Zion's Cooperative Mercantile Institution (ZCMI), the LDS church-owned department store in Salt Lake City. When his father was twenty-four, he was appointed manager of the Deseret Woolen Mills by Brigham Young. The enterprise never succeeded as well as Brigham had hoped. At the death of the patriarch, his son inherited the mill as part of the family estate and ran it with "woefully insufficient capital." The family had to farm on the side to make ends meet. The birth of twin sons, Wladmir and Winfield, added to the family's financial strain. In addition, Agnes's mother, Ellen Nightingale Mackintosh, whose husband had passed away, lived with them.

The Factory, 1903

GRAPHITE ON PAPER, 7″ X 13″
(© COURTESY MUSEUM OF ART, BRIGHAM
YOUNG UNIVERSITY. ALL RIGHTS RESERVED.)

*Throughout his life Young made several
drawings of the factory, of which this is the
earliest. "While Grannie was still alive I
tried to make a drawing of [the] house and
barn from the road as you approach it.
I still have the pencil drawing I made
then. I remember the door into the
enclosure along side of the double
gates used by the teams."*

Oblivious to his family's financial difficulties, Hon loved the factory. His stubborn, independent nature first became evident there when his parents forbade him to go beyond the factory gate because of nearby Parley's Creek. Especially dangerous in the spring and early summer, mountain snow run-off made the stream swollen and swift. One day, when the small child was missing, Agnes found him at the water's edge. Hoping to teach him a lesson, she grabbed the boy and dunked him in the cold water. When she pulled him out, he gasped and called out, "More heady Mama!" meaning that he wanted to be dunked in the water again.[13] Agnes came to believe that her son was incorrigible; others agreed. His desire to be free characterized his entire life and work.

During the child's fifth year, his father instilled an idea that awakened a passionate interest in art and introduced him to the craft that would later become his profession. The boy had become ill

Loading Hay in a Farm Yard

with appendicitis, but no operation was performed. Instead of rupturing the appendix, the infection was allowed to abscess and discharge through his back. To amuse him during his long recovery, his father carved finely-modeled wooden toys. Hon wanted to carve something, as well, but his father did not feel comfortable giving a five-year-old a sharp knife. Instead he brought clay from the

cutbank near their home, out of which the boy modeled small birds and animals.[14] His obvious gift delighted his mother, who hoped to see him develop this talent. She would later extend financial assistance from her meager resources to enable him to study in New York and Paris.

Throughout his life, Hon had a deep love of animals, which he attributed to his father's influence. At the factory he remembered two draft horses and two trotters, as well as cows and chickens and two prized retrievers. The factory's physical setting also had a strong impact. Nestled at the foot of the Wasatch range, it offered mountains rising steeply and majestically to the east, while the

Plowing the Salt Lake Valley, CA. 1920S
OIL ON CANVAS, 29″ X 72″
(© COURTESY MUSEUM OF ART, BRIGHAM YOUNG UNIVERSITY. ALL RIGHTS RESERVED.)

This was a favorite subject for Young. He sculpted, drew, and painted this theme many times throughout his career.

vista of the valley floor and the Great Salt Lake spread out magnificently to the west.

In those days a trip to town was an all-day affair that, for a young child, was a memorable experience. It was six miles by horse and buggy, and more often than not Hon rode with his father in front while Grannie and Agnes rode in back with the younger twins Wally and Winnie on their laps. One could imagine that, to pass the time, the father pointed out the peculiarities of the surrounding countryside. These trips provided a constantly-changing landscape: willows by the creek bed, wild roses along the roadside, cattails and rushes east of Liberty Park, and, from atop Sugar House Hill, the whole valley floor spreading out before them with sage-covered flats sprinkled with patches of yellow sunflowers.

Even though their time together was limited, the father instilled in the son a love of nature. He learned to be observant and to delight in the grand beauty surrounding them. The artist later wrote of the factory:

> It was a place to dream of and regret. There were farmers and a farm; there were workmen and working women at the mill; there were animals and birds in and around the barn; and, in all directions, glorious landscapes. There was clay in the cutbank of the "Dugway." Some of this I was early given to play with and I modeled birds and animals as any child would. . . . When I now get homesick it is always for this part of Salt Lake Valley, for the old adobe blockhouse, the cat-birds, the sunflowers, and the blue mountains forming the rich background.[15]

The "regret" was the untimely death of his father who suffered from inflammatory rheumatism and heart disease. His father had often lain sick in bed for extended periods of time. Late in 1883, when his condition worsened, the family was forced to move into Salt Lake City for the winter where they stayed with relatives at the home of Agnes's uncle, John T. Caine, a Utah territorial delegate to the United States Congress. The family expected to return to the factory, but during the winter Mahonri senior's condition steadily grew worse. Early in the spring of 1884 he passed away at age thirty-two. Mahonri junior wrote about the experience:

> There came a day in the spring of 1884 when I was told to go in and see him. I distinctly remember the darkened room, the distance from the door by which I entered, and his lying in bed. I remember as distinctly as if it were only yesterday standing by his bedside and his talking with me. Oh, how I wish I could remember what he said; but, that's gone! . . . though so much of that visit is still so vivid and distinct. At the time I did not know that I was saying goodby to [him]— that I was seeing him for the last time. [Or] that he knew he had only a few hours left.
>
> Then, I don't know whether it was days or only hours, but we were playing in the front of the big house under a large open day, with the sun shining brightly, and all full of life, spring and youth and happiness, when someone came up to me—someone dressed black, and told me that my father had died. I was old enough to know what that meant. There on the gravel walk, in front of the big stairs in the bright sunlight, I screamed, I cried, I jumped up and down in the agony of grief. Then I remember no more until the day of the funeral. . . .
>
> But, O the memories! I have just gone through it all again, writing this with tears in my eyes and crying in my heart.
>
> From that moment on B Street on that sunny day of June, all life changed for me. Everything from then on was different. In most everything I did the memory of the image of my father was present. When I remembered him his clear physical image came up before me; I could see him as clearly as if he were present. This persisted until I was

about twenty. From then on it became dimmer and vague. It is years now since I could see him.[16]

Hon never returned to the factory, for with his father's death his mother was forced to sell the mill and move to the city. Yet Hon's memory of the factory lived on. He felt that there his father first stirred in him the desire to become a sculptor. In return, he considered his success a tribute to his father's memory.

Years later Mahonri acknowledged how his artistic drive and basic character were formed during those first seven years of his life.[17] In response to the influence the factory had on his art, he wrote:

I was thrown into the company of a number of workmen of many occupations and trades, at the Factory, besides men and women working in the mill itself there was a comp[l]ete farm with all the animals, horses, cows, chickens, that go with a working farm and besides an orchard. I was exposed to the influence of all these different and varied activities and occupations from my most impressionable years. How could I not help but be impressed.[18]

His own son, Mahonri Sharp Young, noted that although his father lived most of his adult life in the East, he always considered himself "a child of the West."[19]

Notes

1. Mahonri M. Young, "Mackintosh Family," Mahonri Young Collection, Mss. 4, box 6, folder 26, Archives and Manuscripts, Harold B. Lee Library, Brigham Young University, Provo, Utah.

2. Young, "Young, Grandma, (Clara Decker)," box 7, folder 31.

3. See George Reynolds and Janne M. Sjodahl, *Commentary on the Book of Mormon* (Salt Lake City: Deseret Book Co., 1977), 5:69. Mahonri Young relates the same account in his personal papers and in the *Juvenile Instructor* 27:282; Young, "Young, Mahonri Moriancumer," box 7, folder 32.

4. Young, "Mahonri," box 6, folder 29.

5. In Dean C. Jessee, ed., *Letters of Brigham Young to His Sons* (Salt Lake City: Deseret Book Co., 1974), 213-14.

6. Young, "Young, Mahonri Moriancumer."

7. *The Salt Lake Tribune*, 29 Aug. 1950; Young, "Etching," box 5, folder 51; Young, "Mahonri," box 6, folder 29.

8. "The artist's account of his only meeting with Brigham Young," *The Salt Lake Tribune*, 20 Aug. 1950; Young, "Young, Brigham," box 7, folder 30.

9. Young, "Notes at the Beginning," in *Mahonri M. Young: Retrospective Exhibition* (Andover, MA: Addison Gallery of American Art, 1940).

10. Leonard J. Arrington, *Great Basin Kingdom: Economic History of the Latter-Day Saints, 1830-1900* (Lincoln: University of Nebraska Press, 1958), 121.

11. Nothing remains of the Deseret Woolen Mills today. It is now the site of the Salt Lake Golf and Country Club.

12. Young, "Notes at the Beginning," box 6, folder 42.

13. Young, "The Factory," box 5, folder 54.

14. Young, "Notes at the Beginning."

15. Ibid.

16. Ibid.

17. Young, "Notes at the Beginning," *Mahonri M. Young,* 47.

18. Young, "Millet, J. F.," box 6, folder 35.

19. Mahonri Sharp Young, *Brigham Young University and M. Knoedler and Company Inc. present an exhibition of sculpture, painting, and drawing of Mahonri M. Young from the Brigham Young University Art Collection, 1969* (n.p., 1969).

CHAPTER THREE.

C Street

*Hon Young's greatest talent was his gift of friendship
for his friends of boyhood days. And those of his boyhood days who had become
superb artists and draughtsmen he loved dearly.*

—Jack Sears

With the death of Young's father in 1884, the family's circumstances changed. The local woolen industry had been in a state of decline for years, and, rather than run the Deseret Woolen Mills by herself, Agnes Young sold the business. She moved her family to a small cottage located at 174 C Street in Salt Lake City's avenues district. Mahonri ("Hon") hated to leave the factory and said he disliked this "respectable part of town."[1] However, city life provided previously unavailable opportunities, not the least of which was formal education. As soon as possible his mother enrolled him in Mrs. Warren's children's school, which met at the teacher's home. There his education began with the basics where he said he was taught the "three R's." After the freedom of country life at the factory, he disliked this restrictive environment.[2]

He then began first grade in the Twentieth Ward School held at the local Latter-day Saint meetinghouse. Learning was difficult for Mahonri. Penmanship, which was required of all students, frustrated him the most. He found that if he wrote backhand he could form letters that were open enough to be acceptable, but his teachers disallowed this. He was embarrassed to find himself at eight years of age the oldest in his class—two grade levels behind most children—and not doing well.

Constant teasing added to his feelings of inferiority. The heckling led to school-yard fights until he won a scrape with the biggest bully. Thereafter his reputation was enhanced among his peers and the teasing about his name and age decreased. School, however, remained nothing more than a chore to be endured. He went through "hating it all the way."[3] He later commented that Miss Alta Wiggins, a large woman with a big heart, taught him the most useful thing he ever learned: when you draw a straight line, you look at the point where the line is going to end and not at the point of the pencil. "Nothing my

MAHONRI YOUNG AT ABOUT AGE 18
(PHOTOGRAPHIC ARCHIVES,
HAROLD B. LEE LIBRARY,
BRIGHAM YOUNG UNIVERSITY,
PROVO, UTAH)

work famous teachers ever taught me had anything like the value of this remark."[4]

Impulsive and fiercely independent, Young chafed at the confinement. His teachers considered him lazy and unfocused. Instead of concentrating on his work, he would look around the room daydreaming. Clearly he would rather be somewhere else, especially outside. He loved sports and acquired a reputation as a good athlete. Local Latter-day Saint congregations sponsored sports events for youth. Because the Youngs were part of the Twentieth Ward congregation, he played on their baseball team. The boys practiced on a vacant lot adjoining Eighteenth Ward Square, later determined to belong to his family through an inheritance from the Brigham Young estate. There they played baseball in the spring and summer as well as football in the fall. At a baseball game between the Twentieth and the Fourteenth wards, Hon met Jack Sears who became a lifelong friend as well as a fellow successful artist.[5]

During these years, Hon loved hunting and fishing and went camping with friends and relatives as often as he could. Anything having to do with nature interested him. At every opportunity he spent time outside, often with a sketchbook. Jack Sears wrote:

> [A canal] ran from east to west along Fourth Street. The banks of this canal served as a haven for many youngsters. Mahonri lived nearby. He and his pals spent many hours lolling on the grassy banks swapping yarns about pioneers, Indians and Indian fighters. . . . Usually when Mahonri returned home he had possessions which his pals lacked—sketches of his friends in action as they romped about the canal, or, as they lay sprawled out upon the grass, daydreaming. Mahonri intended to be an artist, and the drawings he made were done with great care and earnest observation.[6]

His earliest recollection of his father was his return from a successful hunting trip to Utah Lake with a large number of ducks. According to family tradition, the first word young Mahonri ever spoke was "gun."[7]

At twelve or thirteen he obtained his first gun, though this was against the expressed wishes of his mother. Behind her back, he traded with a friend for a .22-caliber rifle, which he hid behind a door in the hallway. He felt guilty for deceiving her but kept the gun and soon became an excellent marksman.

Young also developed an interest in tools. He spent hours at Reister Wright's carpenter shop. Wright, the father of fellow artist Alma Wright, was a master carpenter and one of the best stair builders in the territory. Stern and strict, he usually never allowed anyone in his shop. After a time Mahonri was allowed in and Wright eventually let

The Spire of the 18th Ward Chapel, CA. 1897
GRAPHITE ON PAPER, 4 1/2″ x 6″
(MSS. 4, SKETCHBOOK 27, PHOTOGRAPHIC
ARCHIVES, HAROLD B. LEE LIBRARY,
BRIGHAM YOUNG UNIVERSITY, PROVO, UTAH)

the lad take care of and use his tools. Young started buying his own carpentry tools instead of guns, and soon had a fair collection.[8]

His dislike for school was tempered by an intellectual curiosity. Two people profoundly influenced him during these years: his paternal uncle Alfales and aunt Ada. Both were well educated, and Hon later said he learned more at his uncle's and aunt's home than he ever did in school. In many ways Alfales became a father figure. He was editor of the *Salt Lake Herald*, had attended law school at the University of Michigan, and had such a large personal library that it threatened to take over the house. The boy spent hours browsing through the books and magazines. He was impressed with Ralph Waldo Emerson, Omar Khayyam, and Michel de Montaigne, and for many years he kept a volume of Montaigne's essays by the bedside.[9] The artist's son, Mahonri Sharp Young, later stated that his father's habit of reading, "which he kept up all his life, provided the raw material for his knowledge and his memory. Many a good judge said that he was the best informed man he had ever met. Outside art, his range was phenomenal, and his depth Johnsonian. It was never safe to assume he did not know the answer."[10]

Through his uncle, Hon became acquainted with *Harper's, Scribner's,* and *The Century* magazines, which published articles on famous artists and included examples of their work. In an article in *Scribner's,* Young discovered Jean-François Millet, an artist who would later become a significant influence:

> Since those early days when Millet discovered for me form, space, light, and movement, I have never ceased to love and admire his work, and the more I have studied it and the more I have seen of it the greater and more profound it has become. Though

I studied him, I did not try to imitate him. He sent me to nature and there everywhere were form, space, movement, light and above all life . . .[11]

Time spent with his aunt and uncle resulted in more than an introduction to books. Ada and Alfales were amateur naturalists—Alfales, an avid bird watcher, and Ada, a botanist. They took Hon with them to the canyons east of Salt Lake City to observe the flora and fauna. There he learned to examine nature closely and developed a keen eye and attention to detail, which later found expression in his art.[12]

Other experiences also stimulated his love of the out-of-doors. When the boy expressed an interest in ranching, Oscar Young, another of his many uncles, invited his nephew to spend summers working on his ranch. Hon found this kind of life appealing. More than once he considered the possibility of becoming a rancher if he could not realize his goals in art. But his mother objected after her impulsive son roped a horse while riding bareback and was pulled from his mount and dragged.

Hon had the good fortune to encounter other youngsters in his own neighborhood who shared his creative interests. Some of them went on to become prominent Utah artists: Lee Greene Richards, Alma G. Wright, John Held, Jr., Mary Teasdale, and Jack Sears. These friends greatly influenced each other and remained close throughout their lives.[13] Years later these artists were referred to as the "Twentieth Ward Gang."

The boys were especially close. Together they shared their plans and schemes to accomplish them. Art supplies were often hard to find in Salt Lake City, and Jack Sears's father, Semptius Sears, who managed a ZCMI store, special-ordered them for these youngsters at a good price.[14] Lee Greene Richards's parents shared artistic interests. Mrs.

Julius Caesar, 1890
WOOD, 3″
(© COURTESY MUSEUM OF ART,
BRIGHAM YOUNG UNIVERSITY.
ALL RIGHTS RESERVED.)

Richards was a watercolorist and Mr. Richards owned a copy of Chapman's *American Drawing Book*, which the boys spent hours going through. This book contained fine illustrations, including wood engravings and etchings of works of the great masters, which introduced Young to the art of print-making.[15]

When he was thirteen years old, Mahonri's mother bought him a woodcarving set at ZCMI for fifty cents. The boy immediately set to work on his first sculpture, a four-inch bas-relief of Julius Caesar carved from a piece of old fence post. Although it was crude by professional standards, Mahonri's family and friends considered it an accomplishment. One day a book salesman came to the house and saw it on the mantle. Hearing that a thirteen-year-old boy had carved it, he remarked that the child must be a genius. The epithet stuck and for a time the family referred to him as "the genius."[16]

While living on C Street, Mahonri also developed a strong visual image of pioneer lore that stayed with him throughout his life. He saw visitors come from outlying settlements to Salt Lake City, the center of the Great Basin, to attend church conferences or to resupply and visit friends and relatives. Wagons and teams camped in the Richardses' yard. He listened intently to conversations that inevitably turned to land, crops, and especially water—all reminiscent of the pioneer life of his grandfather's time.[17]

Although raised a Mormon and proud of his heritage, as an adult Young never considered himself a practicing, or "active," member of the church. He dropped out of activity as a teenager. According to Young, his disaffection began during these years on C Street. Fifty years later, as he wrote about his Mormon background in preparation for his projected autobiography, he included a few examples of his early impressions.

Hon's neighbor and friend, Lee Greene Richards, was the son of Lula Louisa Richards, whose piety was pretentious, according to Young. He believed that it was at her insistence that her husband took a second wife to do household chores so she could devote full time to her religion. As the first wife, she ruled over the second, which, to Young's way of thinking, was an injustice that was too common in polygamy. He also thought that Mrs. Richards tyrannized her children. Once, before going swimming in City Creek, Lee's mother expected him to pick gooseberries, which he did with Hon's help, who pitched in to hurry things along. When Mrs. Richards learned of Hon's participation, she told Lee he could not go swimming after all, since she had told him to pick the berries and had not authorized assistance. Angry, Hon threw his gooseberries all over the garden and

stomped off. Later he said that few things ever gave him as much satisfaction as that one rebellious act in protest of a perceived wrong.[18]

Though he was a grandson of Utah's most famous polygamist, Mahonri's impressions came from observing four families living in the neighborhood. As a result of the federal government's attempts to end plural marriage, husbands went into hiding, leaving their wives and children alone. Consequently, he never saw the father of one family. The children seemed to be in the same situation as himself, living without a father. He noticed that there were periodic additions to the family, which meant that the father secretly saw the mother. Otherwise he was nowhere to be found. Despite Hon's sympathy for polygamous wives and their offspring, he felt antipathy for plural marriage.[19] Later in life, when someone would ask him if he was a Mormon, he would retort, "Do you mean do I have more than one wife?"[20]

In his late teens, Young had a favorite pub where he enjoyed what he remembered as the best roast beef sandwich and glass of beer in town. He also enjoyed tea, which Lee Richards's grandmother introduced to them. This was before church president Heber J. Grant declared in 1936 that alcohol, coffee, tea, and tobacco were inappropriate for anyone in a church leadership position. Previously such substances had been discouraged but not forbidden.

Lee's mother took a stricter interpretation of the church's "word of wisdom" regarding dietary habits, and Young's liberal views did not set well with her. To remove her son from Mahonri's "evil influence," she arranged for Lee to serve a Latter-day Saint mission at the early age of eighteen years. For both of these young men, who shared the same dreams and aspirations, the separation was traumatic, "the very worst" development, according to Hon. Nevertheless, they remained friends. Richards wrote from England, where he served his mission, about the great art he saw and encouraged Young to study in Paris. The two planned to go there together after Richards's mission, but when the time came, Lula again separated them. She did not want her son traveling with a "sinner." Hon believed that only "a saint and fanatic" could have come up with such a thing.[21]

Without a father, Mahonri had been on his own during his teenage years and became a strong-headed individualist. Managing to finish the eighth grade, and after reading an article on Millet in which the artist was quoted saying that "no one is ever so classical as when he is doing his own thing," Mahonri decided to quit school, get a job, and study art.[22] So in the fall of 1894, at age seventeen, after attending one day of high school, he broke free and went his own way. His mother adamantly objected, as well as his girlfriend, who considered him a failure for leaving. Undaunted, Mahonri believed that if one knew what he wanted to do in life, why not go ahead and do it?[23]

That same year he suffered a serious accident during a weekend football game. Shoved from behind as he ran to return the ball, his left arm was badly broken. After a doctor set the arm, the splint slipped, causing his arm to begin to heal out of position. Later it had to be forcefully straightened and reset. From that time on, his left arm remained smaller and weaker than his right arm. Considering the physical nature of sculpting, the artist had to contend with this disability throughout his life.[24]

Notwithstanding the injury, he stood up to Sid Lambourne, the toughest kid in town, during a baseball game the next spring. Lambourne, the opposing pitcher, balked in an attempt to pick runners off

base, and Young pointed out the infraction. Infuriated at the challenge, Lambourne threatened him, whereupon Young baited him to carry out his threat. Lambourne came at him with a long right lead, throwing the same punch repeatedly. It landed only the first time. Young used his weakened left arm to block the swings and countered with rights of his own. Lambourne finally conceded, saying this was the only bout he ever lost. In this context, it is interesting that boxing later found expression in some of Young's most successful sculptures.[25]

With his decision to quit school, Young resolved to become an artist like those he had studied in his uncle's magazines. His ambition turned his attention to illustration. His idols were Charles Dana Gibson and Arthur B. Frost. He had seen Frost's illustrations in R. K. Munkritick's book *Farming*. The book first came to his attention through Alan Lovey who worked for the *Salt Lake Herald* as a newspaper cartoonist, and Mahonri repeatedly visited Lovey to see the book and study Frost's illustrations. The book remained a favorite throughout Young's life. He later wrote that he spent years trying to locate one for himself. Everywhere he went, all over the country and in Europe, he searched old bookstores hoping to find one. After thirty years he finally acquired what he sought in a used book store on Fourth Avenue in New York City. A few days later he located a second copy which he gave to his boyhood friend, Jack Sears.[26] Young first saw Gibson's illustrations in Alfales Young's library. Later Mahonri found a book of Gibson's work in the basement library of the old LDS church Social Hall. He checked the book out often and studied the illustrations carefully.[27]

Young found opportunities for art instruction limited. He applied to the art program at the University of Utah, but he was denied because he had attended only one day of high school. Angered and disheartened, he saw little opportunity to study elsewhere until James T. Harwood opened an art school in town. Harwood was one of the most prominent and accomplished Utah artists of the time and had recently returned from studying at the Académie Julian and the Ecole des Beaux Arts in Paris. When Young heard about Harwood's class, he recognized this as a great opportunity. But he could not enroll immediately because he needed money for tuition. He found a job knocking plaster off old bricks from a demolished building. Later he worked at Albion Caine's bicycle, stationary, and curio shop on Second West for $2.50 a week. After two and one-half months, he had enough money to study with Harwood.[28]

One of the first artists from Utah to study in France, James T. Harwood had the added distinction of being the first artist from Utah to have had his work accepted at the coveted Paris Salon art show. In reality Utah had an unusual number of accomplished artists, which was probably due to Brigham Young's early patronage. In 1872 C. C. A. Christensen, an early Utah artist, said, "I would never have believed so much talent could be found among us as a people who are nearly all gathered from among the most downtrodden classes of mankind."[29] Utah historian Edward W. Tullidge said in 1886 that the "early taste and love for pictures in the community was far in advance of that in surrounding territories and greater than the newness of the country would seem to promise." He cited two reasons for this development: first, a larger-than-average proportion of Old World immigrants; and second, the stability of the population. Rather than transient gold seekers and adventurers, Mormons were permanent settlers who gathered to "Zion" with the intent to stay.[30]

Early Utah artists, in particular Dan Weggeland and G. M. Ottinger, taught a whole generation[31] of young people who they encouraged to study in the established art centers of the East and Europe. In 1888 Harwood was joined at the Académie Julian by another Utahn, Cyrus Dallin. In 1890 the Mormon church sent John Hafen, J. B. Fairbanks, and Lorus Pratt on painting missions to France with the understanding that afterwards they would produce the murals for the Salt Lake temple.[32] Of this generation of artists, Harwood and Dallin would have the greatest influence on the early career of Mahonri Young.

Cyrus Dallin, the first Utah-born artist to attain national prominence, showed Young what could be achieved in sculpture. Their paths would cross more than once, and Young's career, patterned on Dallin's, often parallelled the older gentleman's work. Ironically the younger artist later secured important commissions in Utah that Dallin had hoped for.

Born in 1861 in Springville, Utah, the son of early Mormon immigrants, Dallin showed talent at age twelve when he modeled a clay bust of a playmate. He sculpted portrait busts of the founder of the Mormon church, Joseph Smith, and his brother Hyrum, who died as martyrs for their religion. He conceived the idea when he saw their death masks in a travelling show conducted by Philo Dibble, a one-time bodyguard to Joseph Smith. On a later trip Dibble saw the boy's sculptures and was so impressed that he reportedly predicted that Dallin one day would "make figures or busts of Joseph and Hyrum for the Temple,"[33] a prophecy Dallin repeatedly tried to bring to fulfillment.

As his parents had little money, Dallin took various jobs to raise funds to study art at Brigham Young Academy. However, an incident that occurred in the spring of 1879, at age seventeen, changed his life. While working in his father's silver mine thirty miles from Springville, miners struck a vein of soft white clay. Dallin used this clay to sculpt live-sized busts of a man and a woman, then exhibited his work at the territorial fair in the fall, where it attracted considerable attention. Well-to-do mining officials who saw his work said that he should receive professional training in the East and provided him with financial assistance.

In 1880 Dallin was sent to study in Boston with sculptor Truman H. Bartlett. He progressed rapidly, but within the year his money ran out so he took a full-time job at a terra cotta works and sculpted a few commissions on the side. His skills improved and he found employment carving cemetery statues and reliefs for a granite company in Quincy, Massachusetts. At this point he established his own studio and secured a few small commissions. The next year he became one of three finalists in the competition for the now famous equestrian statue of Paul Revere in Boston.

Dallin returned to Utah in 1884. With a rich history and leaders to memorialize, he felt that Utah was primed to commission sculptures and monuments. Recognizing an opportunity to cultivate patronage with the Mormon church, he hoped for a commission to sculpt the church's founders. Unfortunately the church was financially strapped due to national pressure to end polygamy. Church leaders were in hiding and their assets threatened.

Turning to small portrait busts to stimulate interest in his work, Dallin sculpted a statuette of Brigham Young, which he exhibited along with pieces from Boston in one of the main stores in Salt Lake City. To his chagrin, although well received by the public, the show did not lead to any commissions.

Frustrated and disappointed, he returned to Boston where he won the commission for the Paul Revere Statue, signing the contract on the 4th of July 1885. Soon he set his mind to raising enough funds to study in Paris, hoping to complete the commission there, but until he could study abroad he continued in Boston, focusing on heroic images of the American Indian. In 1888 the *Indian Hunter* won a gold metal at the American Art Association show in New York. That same year he realized his dream of going to Paris, arriving soon after Harwood. There he studied with Michel Chapu at the Académie Julian, completing two important works that brought him critical acclaim: the equestrian statue, *Lafayette* and *Signal of Peace* for which he won an honorable mention at the Paris Salon.

After studying abroad, Dallin returned to Boston, married Vittoria Murry, and brought his bride to Utah. Again he hoped for a commission to sculpt statues of Joseph and Hyrum Smith, so he set up a studio in Salt Lake City where he sculpted busts of other prominent Mormons: church president Wilford Woodruff and counselors George Q. Cannon and Joseph F. Smith. Impressed with his work, the church asked him to do a statue of the angel Moroni for the main spire of the nearly-completed Salt Lake temple. At first Dallin refused, saying that he did not feel comfortable with such a commission since he did not believe in angels. At the persuasion of his mother, he accepted. On 6 April 1892, at the church's semi-annual conference, workers put in place the capstone of the temple and installed the Angel Moroni Statue.

The church then wanted Dallin to create a monument to Brigham Young and the pioneers. In January 1892 he began work on the central figure of the monument, but the church lacked funds for casting until 1893 when Dallin was able to complete the over-life-sized figure of Brigham Young in time to exhibit it at the World's Fair in Chicago (the Columbian Exhibition). The remaining sculptures remained unfinished until 1897, and the reliefs were not cast until 1900.[34]

Dallin was never completely satisfied with the Brigham Young Monument. He had to abide by decisions made by a committee that weakened the work's artistic integrity. Alice M. Horne, one of the earliest writers on the arts in Utah, commented in 1914 that the Brigham Young Monument was overseen by "real-estate agents" and "sausage grinders." Regarding Dallin's frustration, she wrote:

> [I]n order to compromise his ideas with those who had the power to dictate, he was forced to sacrifice art. No one is so sure of his own good taste and judgement on art matters and no one is so sure that his ideas are better than the artist's as the man who totally lacks knowledge and feeling for art. If you want a roasting criticism on a good work of art find a person who has no knowledge of these things and he will give ample satisfaction . . . Why will we rob the artist of his finest tool—artistic conception?[35]

Failing to receive the commission to sculpt Joseph and Hyrum Smith, Dallin left Salt Lake City and in 1900 settled permanently in Boston. The commissions he sought would fall to his successor and admirer, Mahonri Young.

But that lay in the future. For now Mahonri was concerned with learning all he could from Harwood, who held classes on the top floor of the Spencer Clawson Building in downtown Salt Lake City. Harwood was assisted by Edwin Evans and John Hafen, all three prominent artists. Young joined students he already knew—Alma Wright, Jack Sears, and Lee Greene Richards.

Their instructors taught classes in the traditional manner of the French Academy, which they "faithfully passed on to us," beginning with the basics of drawing and anatomy.[36] Young's first exposure to anatomy came from a set of anatomical illustrations belonging to John Hafen that included examples by Leonardo da Vinci and Michelangelo. Impressed by the draftsmanship of the old masters, Young realized the importance of anatomy studies and took his drawing seriously. Following the academic tradition, Harwood required that students draw from a plaster cast until they became proficient enough to progress to a live model. Because of the initial unavailability of models, students themselves took turns posing for each other. Finally Harwood hired a female. About this experience, Young reminisced: "How these three dignified men, in Salt Lake, ever found a female model to pose nude is beyond my comprehension, but they did and there she was without a strip on, posing for the three dignified professors and a few students. . . . I remember the talk as to the moral status of the model and the gossip about her."[37]

With Harwood, Young received a solid foundation for future training in New York City and Paris. He also had his first experience in working with modeling clay, the highlight of his classwork there. At the time Dallin was in Salt Lake City working on the Brigham Young Statue, the central figure for the Brigham Young Monument. One day a fellow student, Earl Cummings, brought to class some French modeling clay left over from Dallin's work. This was the first Young had used since his father had brought him clay from the cutbank at the factory. He and Cummings fashioned armatures. With plaster casts as subjects, they sculpted various works. "I made a full sized study of a mask of the *Laocoön*, and some details from Michelangelo's *David*. We then tried Carpeau's *Laughing Faun*." Although they were not trained in sculpture, Young's

John Hafen, CA. 1894

GRAPHITE ON PAPER, 7″ X 4 1/2″
(MSS. 4, SKETCHBOOK 27,
PHOTOGRAPHIC ARCHIVES,
HAROLD B. LEE LIBRARY,
BRIGHAM YOUNG UNIVERSITY,
PROVO, UTAH)

Leda Stromberg, Woman of Distinction, CA. 1898
PEN AND INK ON PAPER, 12″ x 9″
(MUSEUM OF CHURCH HISTORY AND ART,
THE CHURCH OF JESUS CHRIST OF LATTER-DAY SAINTS,
SALT LAKE CITY, UTAH)

B. H. Roberts, Democratic Nominee for Congress, 1897-98
PEN AND INK ON PAPER, 12″ x 9″
(MUSEUM OF CHURCH HISTORY AND ART,
SALT LAKE CITY)

instructors recognized his talent and natural ability. However, he would not again attempt to sculpt until in Paris.[38]

Harwood considered Lee Richards his best student. Richards was a methodical and careful draftsman, whereas Young had a peculiar approach that caused problems. He worked quickly, in spurts of energy, then spent the remaining time looking around the room. It irked Harwood to see Young "loafing." Young felt that this was because of his teacher's old-fashioned conventions. Harwood was convinced that work made success and that the best students were those who worked long and hard, even though they might make little progress. Young felt that it was no compliment to lavish praise upon a work because the artist had worked hard on it. To him, work was not a virtue but a necessity. Drawings that displayed the artist's struggles, frustrations, and lack of competence, fatigued the beholder. Young believed, like Goethe, that work was the easy part; thinking was hard.[39]

Harwood encouraged his serious students to seek further training in the East and abroad as he had done, and, as a result, Young made up his mind to go to New York and attend the Art Students League. But to study in New York City he would need money. This time, because of his art training, he did not have to find a job doing menial labor. When his drawing skills became good enough, Alfales Young secured him a job as a part-time newspaper sketch artist for the *Salt Lake Herald*. His success there resulted in full-time employment when *The Salt Lake Tribune* hired both him and Jack Sears—Young as a portrait artist for $5 and Sears, who had studied in New York for a year, as a cartoonist for $10 a week. Later Young commented that it was unheard of at that time for two Mormon boys to be working at *The Salt Lake*

Tribune, a newspaper known to represent anti-Mormon positions.[40]

Their work together lasted only a few months. Sears lost his job and Young was demoted to the engraving department when the newspaper hired an artist from Indiana. Instead of drawing, Young now copied the other artist's works to an engraving plate to print in the newspaper. "It was quite a pill to swallow to start at the very bottom as the 'louse' in the engraving department after having been an artist. But I stuck to it for almost four years."[41] He disliked the mechanical aspects of his job. The equipment was poor and the work tedious and difficult. But he decided to "learn the damn job and save every penny."[42] "This was one of the most trying periods of my life. I had determined I was going to go ahead. I realized nobody was going to help me. There was nothing to do but do it all myself."[43] Young went to work at 2:00 in the afternoon and usually finished between 2:00 and 4:00 in the morning. There were benefits, for while working in the engraving department he learned the printmaking and etching process. This marked the beginning of a love for this medium that would last throughout his life and bring him some success and satisfaction. Furthermore the drawings he did for the *Herald* and *Tribune* mark the first major body of art work of Young's career. *Leda Stromberg, Woman of Distinction* and *B. H. Roberts, Democratic Nominee for Congress*, for example, show the obvious influence of one of the most celebrated American illustrators of the period, Charles Dana Gibson. In the pages of these newspapers can be found fine examples of Mahonri's early artistic skills and technical ability. His training during this period in many ways parallels the early careers of Robert Henri and the Group of Eight in New York City, most of whom started as newspaper artists.

During this time Young began formulating ideas about art which would eventually lead him to associate with such realist painters as Henri and the Ashcan school and to reject the classical, laborious practice of drawing meticulously from plaster casts and models. Having worked as a newspaper sketch artist, Young became adept at doing quick drawings from life, a technique and skill that his job required. Before photography was adapted to journalism, the newspaper artist recorded visual images of news as it happened. This shorthand method proved to be philosophically at variance with the practice of trained instructors who preferred meticulous work. Academicians like Harwood considered quick-sketch art beneath them. Nevertheless, Young also learned a great deal from Harwood, whom he considered to be his "first and best teacher." He later wrote, "Fortunate, indeed, are we, that in our early years we studied under him and were not only taught to draw correctly, but also to appreciate nature, life and the value of time."[44]

Throughout this trying time Young's ultimate goal was to continue his art training in the East. Since he never had time for entertainment, he found it easy to save money. He lived with his mother, which allowed him to save $5.75 from every weekly paycheck of $6. Soon he had saved over $400, which enabled him to study for almost a full year at the Art Students League in New York.[45]

Just before his departure, his grandmother Mackintosh, who had known religious persecution in the Midwest, warned Mahonri that it would be dangerous to let anyone know that he came from Utah, that his last name was Young, or that he was a Mormon. He decided contrariwise that he would never repudiate his birthplace, ancestry, or heritage, which was a decision he would not come to regret.[46] He was born a Mormon in a territory that was once governed by his grandfather, yet the world beyond Utah was about to provide him with what he needed to achieve his artistic aspirations.

Notes

1. Mahonri M. Young, "Notes at the Beginning," Mahonri M. Young Collection, Mss. 4, box 6, folder 42, Archives and Manuscripts, Harold B. Lee Library, Brigham Young University, Provo, Utah.

2. Young, "One Seventy Four C Street," box 6, folder 43.

3. Young, "Notes at the Beginning," in *Mahonri M. Young: Retrospective Exhibition* (Andover, MA: Addison Gallery of American Art, 1940), 48.

4. Young, "Notes at the Beginning," box 6, folder 42.

5. Young, "Eighteenth Ward Square," box 5, folder 49.

6. In Jack Sears Collection, Mss. 1058, Archives and Manuscripts, Lee Library.

7. Young, "Notes at the Beginning."

8. Young, "Wright, Alma Brockerman," box 7, folder 29.

9. Young, "Books that have influenced me," box 5, folder 13.

10. Mahonri Sharp Young, *Brigham Young University and M. Knoedler and Company Inc. present an exhibition of sculpture, painting, and drawing of Mahonri M. Young from the Brigham Young University Art Collection, 1969* (n.p., 1969).

11. Young, "Notes at the Beginning," box 6, folder 42.

12. Young, "Alfales, Uncle and Ada, Aunt," box 5, folder 2.

13. Sears, "Mahonri Young biographical notes," box 3.

14. Ibid.

15. Young, "Etching," box 5, folder 51.

16. Sears, "Mahonri Young biographical notes."

17. Wayne Kendall Hinton, "A Biographical History of Mahonri M. Young, A Western American Artist," Ph.D. diss., Brigham Young University, 1974, 38.

18. Young, "Richards, Lee Greene," box 7, folder 5.

19. Young, "Eighteenth Ward Square."

20. Young, "Notes at the Beginning."

21. Young, "Richards, Lee Greene."

22. Young, "Farming," box 5, folder 55.

23. Young, "Notes at the Beginning."

24. Young, "Eighteenth Ward Square."

25. Ibid.

26. Young, "Farming."

27. Young, "Vierge," box 7, folder 21.

28. Young, "Caine, Albion (First Job)," box 5, folder 19.

29. James L. Haseltime, *100 Years of Utah Paintings* (Salt Lake City, 1965), 9.

30. Ibid.

31. Ibid., 10.

32. Linda Jones Gibbs, *Harvesting the Light: The Paris Art Mission and Beginnings of Utah Impressionism* (Salt Lake City: The Church of Jesus Christ of Latter-day Saints, 1987).

33. Rell G. Francis, *Cyrus E. Dallin: Let Justice Be Done* (Springville, UT: Springville Museum of Art, 1976), 5.

34. Robert S. Olpin, *Dictionary of Utah Art* (Salt Lake City: Salt Lake Art Center, 1980), 47-57; Francis, *Cyrus E. Dallin.*

35. Alice Merril Horne, *Devotees and Their Shrines: A Handbook of Utah Art* (Salt Lake City: The Deseret News, 1914), 98.

36. Young, "Harwood's Class," box 6, folder 4.

37. Ibid.

38. Ibid.

39. Hinton, 56.

40. Young, "Etching."

41. Young, "Notes at the Beginning."

42. Young, "Etching."

43. Young, "Notes at the Beginning."

44. Young, "Harwood's Class."

45. Young, "Etching."

46. Ibid.

CHAPTER FOUR.

The Bohemian Years: New York City and Paris

The years in Paris were decisive.
He went there as an inexperienced student; he left there a fully-formed artist.

—Mahonri Sharp Young

The four and a half years Mahonri Young spent in New York City and Paris were the most important in his development as an artist— not only in the classroom but in the museums, studios, and in the streets where he encountered poor, urban workers. In France his first bronzes of Parisian laborers signaled the direction the rest of his life's work would take.

Manhattan had developed into a cultural mecca around the turn of the century when Young, along with other artists from around the country, arrived there to study and work. The Metropolitan Museum of Art was collecting some of the country's most important treasures. The Art Students League, where Young chose to attend, drew students who either could not meet the entrance requirements of the National Academy in New York City or disliked the academy's rigid curriculum. The league's student body was highly motivated and the faculty included some of the best talent in America.[1]

About this time, as the nation's values shifted, the arts too changed. In the 1890s impressionism was on the rise in America, especially among academic painters and their wealthy patrons. Younger artists admired American impressionists William Merritt Chase, J. Alden Weir, Theodore Robinson, Childe Hassam, and John Twachtman mostly for their technique, but began to question their idyllic themes and upper-class subject matter. The impressionists for their part considered the new realism, especially the so-called Ashcan school, to be vulgar.

America's long tradition of realism had little to do with the new style that was inspired by the reality of day-to-day life among the working class. The new realism symbolized industrial urban society, and its strongest exponents considered themselves largely free of European influence. Banding together under the leadership of Robert Henri, they called themselves the Group of Eight. Mahonri Young became associated with them. Raised in the

West, and having seen and portrayed all walks of life as a newspaper sketch artist, his own temperament was at odds with traditionalists and more inclined toward raw emotion. For Young, life had not been idyllic. He felt a bond with other working people. Despite the innovation that seemed to be evident everywhere in Europe and America, the French schools and their American counterparts still taught in the Beaux Arts tradition where fine art was to be carefully composed and meticulously rendered. The Group of Eight, like Young, revolted against this style and its academic institutionalism.

Young's trip to New York in the fall of 1899 included a layover in Chicago. This was the first big city he had ever seen and he found it intimidating but rewarding. He traveled the entire way in the train's day coach to save money. Upon arrival, he went immediately to the famous Art Institute:

> While there in Chicago, I hurried to the Institute; that was the first picture gallery I had ever seen. Things were hung differently there then. Two of Delacroix's finest animal studies, a lioness, and a tiger, and another small picture were all hung against a cornice. A superb Courbet mountain landscape occupied a similar position. These pictures were all beautifully displayed when I last saw them a year ago. The great Rembrandt, the "Girl at a Door," was there then and on loan was Millet's little picture of a "Woman Bathing." To me at that time, it seemed a masterpiece of the first order—it still does. I have seen it every time I have passed through Chicago, and it still remains as good as when I first saw it.[2]

This experience marked the beginning of a life-long habit of haunting museums. From that time on he considered them his greatest teachers. He said that for the remainder of the trip all he could think about was getting to New York so he could visit the Metropolitan Museum of Art.

When he arrived, he was met by Janette Eastum, his father's half-sister. New arrivals from Utah often stayed with the Eastums while they established themselves. "Net," as she was called, was a daughter of Brigham Young's wife Clara Decker Young who had traveled with the first pioneer company to Utah, and as such she held a prominent place in Utah society. She married and divorced at an early age and accompanied her second husband, Robert Eastum, when he sought to advance his music career by moving to New York. Having previously gained success as a player at the Salt Lake Theatre, she also hoped to further her career. She loved New York, but she also kept close ties with Salt Lake City and wrote a weekly letter to the *Deseret News* entitled, "Salt Lakers in New York." Mahonri felt that his aunt, a woman with a penchant for earthy stories, was the "truest Bohemian" he had ever known. He stayed with the Eastums until his roommate, Harry Stoddard, arrived, after which they found a room on 63rd and Park Avenue for $12 a month.[3]

On 1 October 1899 Young registered for classes at the Art Students League. He was pleased that the administration considered his studies with James T. Harwood sufficient to allow him into the life drawing class. Anxious to begin, he arrived every weekday morning when the school opened. Classes were conducted in a precise and orderly manner, patterned after the European académies: students came in beginning at 8:00 a.m. and began to set up, at 8:15 a model was posed, the students worked until lunch time, and the instructor arrived later in the morning to critique their work.[4]

Young studied with George B. Bridgeman who had taught Life Drawing and Anatomy at the league since 1894. Known as a fine draftsman, he also wrote and published books on drawing and anatomy, some of which are still in use today. Knowing his reputation as a demanding teacher famous for scathing criticism, Young disliked his method from the beginning. Bridgeman appeared twice a day. After being announced, he entered the room, counted his pupils, then looked at his watch to determine how much time to give each one. He made the rounds giving almost the same criticism to everyone, usually to "get the hip action" or "make it go round."[5] Sometimes he illustrated his point with a small sketch drawn to the side of the student's work. After a short time Young refused to consider himself Bridgeman's student. Feeling he never learned anything from him, he questioned the value of his teacher's presence. Even so, Bridgeman considered Young one of the best in the class and ranked him number one, then number two when the professor's previously favorite student began attending again.[6]

The instructor in Young's afternoon course, Kenyon Cox, had taught at the league from 1884 to 1909. Known as a portrait painter and muralist in the classical tradition, Cox gained prominence as a result of the large murals he executed for the 1893 Columbian Exposition in Chicago. One of America's best muralists, he received other major commissions, including work for the Library of Congress, and emerged as a major figure in the American Renaissance movement. A series of lectures published in 1911 as *The Classic Point of View* made Cox the best-known voice and spokesman for the theories and ideals of academic classicism.

At the school Cox had a reputation as an excellent but exacting instructor. All beginning students under his tutelage began by drawing from plaster casts and advanced to a live model only when Cox thought they were ready. He allowed students to enter competitions only when he felt their work

was good enough. Young studied with him the entire season. Despite the fact that his methods were conservative and controlled, Young learned concepts from Cox that stayed with him his entire life. "He never told me anything which I found out wasn't so. I have always had the sincerest respect for Kenyon Cox."[7] The instructor's ideas and philosophy of art influenced Young's later approach to the human form. About his teacher's interaction with students, Young wrote:

> He proceeded to study the drawings in relationship to the model and indicated corrections. He sometimes made his corrections with a line. In this he carefully ran his charcoal over the drawing from point to point, . . . [making his] line with firmness and assurance. There were no free flowing, finding-out lines. That operation he apparently had made in his mind.[8]

In addition to classes, Cox gave a series of lectures on anatomy which Young found especially instructive. The lectures were geared to the needs of the artist rather than to a purely physiological approach. "He didn't go very far into the deeper muscles . . . his aim being to give an idea of the structure of the figure, not to take it to bits. He explained the articulation of the skeleton and the function of the larger muscles and the ones that determine the form."[9] Cox taught that the artist needed "first, to develop in the highest degree the abstract beauty and significance possessed by lines in themselves, more or less independently of representation: second, to express with the utmost clearness and force the material significance of objects and, especially, of the human body."[10] These theories and ideas had a lasting influence on Young's later work. He strove for what he considered the essential rather than the specific in his art, an

objective he achieved in the finest of his later statues of laborers and prizefighters.

During his studies at the Art Students League,
Young thought of becoming an illustrator. He had
worked as a newspaper artist and admired magazine illustrators, so this was perhaps predictable.
Even though Cox was a personal friend of the prominent sculptor Augustus Saint-Gaudens who had
also previously taught at the league, Young neither
studied nor mentioned experimenting with sculpture in New York.

The theme of labor abounds in Young's New
York sketches. Captivated by the energy he saw in
the city and the new construction everywhere, he
found artworthy scenes all around him. The Vanderbilt Building underway next door to the Art Students League attracted his attention, and he later
wrote that during rest periods in the life drawing
class he and other students looked out the windows
to watch progress on the site. One time Young
observed an Italian workman breaking stones with a
heavy sledge. Fascinated, he called the attention of
another student to the man, professing that one day
he would like to do a statue of him. Young benefit-
ted not only from what was on the model stand but
from what he saw out the window and in the streets
below. He later commented that the inspiration for
one of his most successful sculptures came to him
at this time in New York City.[11]

Later that year Young enrolled in an illustration class taught by Walter Appleton Clarke (1876-
1906), one of the best-known illustrators of the
period whose own career had its beginnings when
he was a student at the league. After seeing some
of the work there, the art editor of *Scribner's* magazine awarded Clarke his first professional commission. Although his career ended abruptly with his
untimely death, Clarke executed many exceptional

magazine covers and memorably illustrated Percy
MacKeye's modern version of Chaucer's *Canterbury
Tales*.[12] He also attended an advanced class taught
by the illustrator Robert Blum.[13]

Of all of his experiences, Young felt that a lecture on landscape painting delivered by the American impressionist John H. Twachtman was the
most rewarding. Although much of impressionism
in America was merely a copy of French style and
technique, Twachtman was one of the few who
brought to America his own unique interpretation.
This was one of the last lectures he delivered, for
the next year he died. More than any other experience, this expanded Young's understanding and
insights into what art could be:

> His talk to us was one of the highlights of my
> year in New York, and gave me more than all
> the rest of the year put together. His lecture
> was just like his standing there and rolling back
> some curtains, and there were vistas that he
> showed us. He spoke of people we were vaguely
> familiar with, but he clarified why they were and
> why they weren't. He was a creative artist who
> thought deeply on his art, talking to us, giving us
> credit for more than we were entitled to, and it
> made a tremendous impression.[14]

Young also attended a lecture course on composition taught by academic painters George de
Forest Brush and Bryson Burroughs which he considered enlightening and beneficial.[15]

Young's accomplishments in those eight
months in New York were remarkable considering the fact that health problems plagued him
constantly. His night job as a newspaper artist for
The Salt Lake Tribune altered his sleeping habits so
much that he still had trouble sleeping nights,
even after studying all day at the league. When he
suffered a long bout with the flu, his aunt Net
nursed him back to health, but to his great concern

The Deseret News, 1903

GRAPHITE ON PAPER, 8 3/4″ x 9 3/4″
(MSS. 4, SKETCHBOOK 27,
PHOTOGRAPHIC ARCHIVES,
HAROLD B. LEE LIBRARY,
BRIGHAM YOUNG UNIVERSITY,
PROVO, UTAH)

he was then plagued by severe headaches. He was greatly relieved when eyeglasses remedied the problem.[16]

Never indulging in luxuries, his drive to learn all he could absorbed him so that he had little desire for anything else. Whenever he was not studying he visited exhibits and museums. When he found he had to return to Utah a month early—in eight months rather than nine—he was physically and financially exhausted.

Despite the difficulties, he felt rewarded and decided to resume his studies as soon as possible in Paris. At the turn of the century, Paris was the center of the art world and every serious student hoped to study there. The Académie Julian, which was popular with Americans, was established for the purpose of accommodating the ever-growing number of foreigners. Its open enrollment policy made it accessible to Americans, and this is where Young decided to continue his training.

The most prestigious academy was Ecole des Beaux Arts, but it was expensive and the entrance requirements were difficult and competitive. A popular option was the Académie Julian. The académie's founder, M. Julian, had studied art for years but had no particular skill or originality. In fact, his only significant success was opening his académie. Classes ran all day from 7:00 a.m. or 8:00 a.m. until 5:00 p.m. Two live models posed simultaneously at each end of the room, as students meticulously drew in charcoal, pencil, or pen.[17]

Young was influenced by his friend, Lee Richards, who had just completed a proselyting mission for the Mormon church in England. At the conclusion of his mission, Richards toured France where he visited museums, sketched, and talked with American art students. In letters to Young, he urged his friend to study there.[18] When Richards returned from England and Young from New York, they finalized their plans to take classes and room together in France.

In order to do this, they both needed money, so Young returned to his old job as a newspaper illustrator and engraver for the *The Salt Lake Tribune*. Because he had studied in the East, the pay was better now. He received $18 a week, supplemented by free-lance work for the *Deseret News*. Although he scrimped and saved over $500 that year, he still did not have enough until he obtained an additional $500 from the sale of a piece of property, the same lot where he had played ball as a child, the Eighteenth Ward Square. Mahonri's mother believed that the church owned the land, but in 1900 she learned that it had been given to her husband as part of Brigham Young's estate.[19] She asked the church for a settlement; President Lorenzo Snow offered so little that she refused. In October 1901 Joseph F. Smith became president of the church. She again asked for a settlement. This time the full market value was offered, so the family accepted. As Young later recorded: "They were willing to settle with us especially as our portion was to be used for education. President Joseph F. Smith turned over to my mother our share. This allowed my brother Wladmir to go back to Stanford; my other brother Winfield Scott allowed me to use his share so that with what I had saved I had something over $1000. With this I started for Paris."[20]

He left for Paris in late 1901, beginning with a long train ride to Boston where he was to board a ship to Liverpool. During a three-hour layover in Buffalo, New York, he went straight to the art pavilion. There he saw the work of J. Alden Weir for the first time, several watercolors by Winslow Homer, and recent sculptures by Cyrus Dallin. He had followed Dallin's career with interest and hoped that he would soon have the opportunity to meet him in Boston where he resided.

When his ship was delayed for a few days, Young arranged a meeting with Dallin. He found him to be warm, cordial, and encouraging, and since he had recently returned from studying in Paris, they talked for hours. "Dallin gave me such priceless advice that I still value. The things he said to me were, study the old masters and . . . [in art] general truths are more valuable than particular ones."[21]

In Liverpool Young sketched the activities of the crowded streets of this English port. He considered watching the people there "better than a Vaudeville show."[22] He took a train to London where he visited the British Museum, the National Gallery, and the Tate and Walker galleries, which were vast and important collections that made American museums and galleries seem insignificant by comparison.

He arrived in Paris six weeks later than originally planned. By this time Richards was already attending the Académie Julian and had found an apartment and roommates.[23] Needing to make other arrangements, Young moved into a studio at 7 rue Relline with Howard McCormick, a former friend from the Art Students League. Rustic at best, their studio apartment was constructed from materials salvaged from the 1900 World's Fair and lacked such basics as drapes or even a couch.[24]

Young enrolled in a drawing class taught by Jean-Paul Laurens. Well-known in the Paris art world, Laurens was a life-long friend and confidant of sculptors Jules Dalou and Auguste Rodin, two artists who would become important influences on Young. Laurens taught in the same manner Young had become familiar with at the Art Students League. Class began at 8:00 a.m. and ended at 5:00

p.m. with an hour break at noon for lunch. At the start of each class a model was posed and the students commenced drawing, and Laurens would later come in to critique their work.[25]

Laurens chose drawings to enter in student competitions, and at first Young's work was consistently chosen for the "concours" but later ignored. Young was puzzled. He wrote:

Jean-Paul [Laurens] would indicate the ones he wanted for the Concours by a nod of the head to Raphael, the man of all work. Jean-Paul seemed to indicate that my drawing was to be marked, but Raphael never seemed to see it. An "Ancient" [who had studied at the academy more than one year] suggested that maybe if I crossed his palm, his eyesight might be better. The next day I said, "Raphael, if Jean-Paul marks my drawing today you get two francs." That was all that was needed. My drawings were marked from then on, but I had to continue crossing the palm.[26]

From the beginning Young did not do as well in drawing as he had hoped and became discouraged. Academic training emphasized tight and controlled technique and meticulously-rendered finished drawings. Constantly struggling with this style of drawing, Young never felt as successful as at the Art Students League. This bothered him. "That's not drawing life," he later wrote. "Life moves. Those fellows are trying to stand still—those models are trying to stand still, and somebody in the class is always yelling at them to hold the pose. They've got to learn when they leave there to draw things that don't pose and are always moving, or they've got to learn to memorize them and draw them afterwards."[27] Over the couse of the year Young spent less time in class and more time visiting the Louvre and Luxembourg museums.

Still his studies in France brought him fresh opportunities and a new circle of influential friends.

Paris Street Scene, 1903
GRAPHITE ON PAPER, 9″ X 7 1/2″
(MSS. 4, SKETCHBOOK 28,
PHOTOGRAPHIC ARCHIVES,
HAROLD B. LEE LIBRARY,
BRIGHAM YOUNG UNIVERSITY,
PROVO, UTAH)

Initially concerned about a language barrier, to his relief he found that students at the academy spoke English, as most were from America and Great Britain. He already knew Richards and McCormick and soon met other students including the American artist Eugene Higgins who impressed Young with his drawings and paintings of society's outcasts. He sensed in Higgins's work a genuine sentiment that he felt must come from personal experience. Young said that Higgins used to say, "I am not melancholy; when I become melancholy I paint a murder and get rid of it that way."[28] Higgins was known as an artist of talent, but, because of his unusual life style, his fellow artists referred to him as a "poor beggar in a garret who paints beggars and miserables because he is one of them."[29]

During this time Young became close friends with two influential men, Alfred H. Maurer and Leo Stein. He met Stein at the academy "where he was trying to draw." Stein first studied in Italy under the famous art historian Bernard Berenson, then moved to Paris to study painting. As beginning students at the academy, they quickly became good friends:

> I have only known one or two men in my life as well informed as he, especially in art. He was still comparatively young, just past thirty, very much alive, interested in everything connected with art, discovering new things in the old and the new and loving to talk about his discoveries. It was later he discovered the modernist. I remember his taking me to see a show by a young Spaniard, named Picasso, held in a furniture store. He was entranced.[30]

Leo's sister Gertrude Stein, the innovative American writer, joined him in Paris in 1903, and by 1906 their apartment had become a meeting place for avant garde artists, among them Matisse

Leo Stein, 1931
TERRA COTTA, 11 1/4″
(© COURTESY MUSEUM OF ART,
BRIGHAM YOUNG UNIVERSITY.

Alfy (A. H. Maurer), 1902
conte on paper, 10″ x 6″
(© courtesy Museum of Art,
Brigham Young University.

and Picasso. Among the first collectors of modern art, the Steins amassed an impressive collection.

These friendships proved to be lifelong. In later years, for example, whenever Mahonri, Leo, and Alfred were together in Paris, they went to lunch regularly at a favorite spot. Before coming to Paris in 1897, Maurer was an academic painter with training from the National Academy in New York City. In 1904, when he became good friends with Gertrude and Leo Stein, he converted to modernism. One of the first Americans to comprehend the art of Matisse and the Fauves, Maurer incorporated similar elements into his work. After Maurer's thirty-sixth birthday, Young said of him, "From that day on he painted like a wild man. He was never the lighthearted, gay Alfy we had known."[31]

It is worth noting that among Young's closest and most enduring friends, Stein and Maurer were influential figures in the history of modernism. These associations intimately acquainted Young with the movement, but he never found himself drawn to it. Throughout his life he expressed only disdain for modern art. Intellectually and emotionally tied to the pioneers of modernism, Young could have been in on the ground level of the avant-garde, but his own avenue of expression remained realism.

During the Easter recess of 1902, a group of students invited Young to travel to Italy with them. No longer the most influential art center, Italy still held a powerful hold on artists, as it had for centuries, as a living museum. At first reluctant because of the cost involved, Young finally decided it would be a valuable learning experience. Most of the students viewed the trip as a vacation; Young considered it an education. During the three weeks he spent there, he visited Venice, Florence, Milan, Padua, and Rome. Thoughout the trip he kept a sketchbook

journal of drawings and notes. Each night he returned to his room to go over his sketches, some of which later inspired a number of important works: "From that most revealing trip I brought back a number of ideas and observations that have been invaluable to me. . . . I discovered that modern pictures were too simple—that is there wasn't nearly as much of interest in them as in the Italian ones. In most Italian pictures . . . there was something to look at wherever one looked."[32] In reviews of Young's later works, critics often compared his work to, and found strong influences from, the masters of the Italian Renaissance whose works were similarly full of life and energy. Undoubtedly their impact on Young during his Italy trip strengthened his resolve to stay with realism.

Young returned to Paris and soon branched out into other mediums, feeling more hopeful about oil painting, which up until this time had been difficult and frustrating. He also started making prints. His previous experience with printmaking as a newspaper artist had taught him much about the technical aspects of the craft, but now he could turn his attention completely to printmaking as an art. His first print, a view of the famous Spanish Steps in Rome, was based on a sketch he had done in Italy. He also completed a print of an unused blacksmith's forge near the apartment he and Alma Wright now shared. *The Forge Rue St. Jacques* was the result. The forge was tucked away in an old dilapidated architectural façade that had been converted to a depot and outlet for coal, wood, and wine. Attracted to the subject since childhood, Young expressed his fascination for forges and farriers. He later wrote, "I didn't go in for such things as blacksmith tools, though I never passed a blacksmith shop without stopping and watching the smith at his work."[33] The work was displayed to favorable response at the first public exhibit of his etchings in 1904.[34]

In the fall of 1902 Young decided to turn to sculpture. After returning from Italy he went with Maurer to Chesey for a short vacation, where he spent time reviewing what he had accomplished and planning his future. Lower in class standing at the Académie Julian than at the Art Students League, he was discouraged with his progress in drawing and no doubt questioned his future as an illustrator. He felt that a change might do him good:

> The next winter I determined to go back to my earliest love, and enter the modeling class at Julian's under Raoul Verlet. After the first month, I never took criticism from M. Verlet. I had no sympathy with his sculpture or his point of view. My studies in the Luxembourg, the Louvre, and the trip to Italy had given me a very different idea of what sculpture should be. In the spring, I modeled, in my studio, my first original work *The Shoveler* followed by *Man Tired*.[35]

Sculpture may have been his earliest love, but this was Young's first sculpture class and the first time he had worked in the medium to any extent. It is interesting that his formal training in sculpture, or in art in general, for the remainder of his stay in Paris was not extensive. From then on he attended a few drawing classes now and then at the Académie Delacluze. Later he studied with Jean-Antoine Injalbert for two or three months at La Grande Chaumiere Académie Colarossi. Young considered Injalbert his greatest teacher and said, "He may not have been a great sculptor but for me, he was much more important—he was a master sculptor in the sense a master plummer is a master plummer, or a master carpenter is a master carpenter, in other words he knew his job."[36]

That same fall Howard McCormick returned to America. At about the same time Al Wright arrived

The Forge Rue St. Jacques, 1902
ETCHING, 7 1/4″ X 5 7/8″

from Salt Lake City, so Young and Wright arranged to share accommodations. They both worked in Young's studio and slept in Wright's apartment. By this time there was quite a group of Utahns studying in Paris. That same year, Louise Richards arrived, joining the ranks of the small colony of former Harwood pupils: Lee Richards, Alma Wright, and Young.

Although this period marks the beginning of Young's sculptures of laborers, in an article published in 1924 Young confirmed that the theme occurred to him as early as 1897.[37] In fact, images of workers appear in many of his early drawings and sketchbooks. Given the artist's background, it is not surprising that he would be drawn to this subject. Work was the lifeblood of pioneer Utah. The theme quickly became his deeply-felt personal statement: "You might say this is my tribute to honest toil."[38]

The theme of labor in Young's art was a natural extension of his life and times. To survive in the Great Basin of the Rocky Mountains, hard work was a way of life—preached from the pulpit and practiced everyday. For Young, this sentiment would find expression in his Sea Gull Monument and culminate in his This is the Place Monument. But hard-working subsistence was more than a pioneer heritage; it was central to life in America, and had already been featured in the paintings of Winslow Homer, Eastman Johnson, and Thomas Eakins, as well as in the poetry of Walt Whitman.[39] At the turn of the twentieth century the country and particularly the East experienced a major upheaval. Emerging as a manufacturing giant after the Civil War, the nation became industrialized, vast fortunes were made, and urban populations were created. To counterbalance the power of corporate management, labor began to assert its

own power. By 1905 the American Federation of Labor reached 1.5 million members, with other labor unions increasing rapidly. Strikes were frequent and the conflicts and inequities brought by industrial growth found expression in art and literature of the period under the banner of naturalism and realism, specifically in the writings of Frank Norris, Stephen Crane, and Theodore Dreiser, and the paintings of the Ashcan school.

During the first decade of the new century alone, nine million people immigrated to the United States. More people meant more construction. In this restless milieu the art that emerged was unrefined and drew its vitality from street life. When Young studied in New York City, this new art was in its infancy. In just over a decade he would return to become a significant American sculptor associated with the Ashcan school.

It was in Europe, however, that Young discovered the artistic potential of common labor—particularly in sculpture. By the end of the nineteenth century the subject was well established in France, having first appeared in French painting and to a lesser extent in sculpture shortly after the revolution of 1848. As a result of the growing influence of labor movements and the size of the labor force, combined with the productivity of the Industrial Revolution, the worker had changed the face of Europe and America. The noble qualities of a simple life and honest work attracted artists.

Painters such as Courbet and Millet produced some of the most famous and memorable images in this genre. Millet's work especially became widely known and popular both in Europe and America. Young became aware of Millet's work through magazine illustrations.

In sculpture, the acceptance and popularity of people doing menial jobs grew more slowly.

Mid-century classical figures appeared with allegorical references to work. For example, a nude female holding a string of fish was meant to represent the work of fishermen. This type of representation remained unchanged for several decades. Allied with the tradition of classical French sculpture and the academic style, these representations had little to do with real life.[40]

It was not until the 1880s that sculptures of working peasants finally began to take on the realism of a Courbet or Millet painting. Allegorical depictions gave way to figures actually doing work. Even after literal depictions replaced classical idealizations, the nude still remained unchallenged as the basic mode of representation. Alfred Boucher's *To the Earth*,[41] exhibited in the Paris Salon of 1890, depicted a nude man in the act of shoveling.

By the last two decades of the century believable images, contemporary figures, authentic in dress and realistic in pose, began to appear in France and the rest of Europe. In Italy as early as 1880 D'Orsi's *Proximus Tuus* and Vela's *The Victims of Labor* in 1882 preceded the continental trend. However, it was the Belgian artist Constantin Meunier who first gained international attention. Meunier began his career as a painter, although he was also trained in sculpture. Primarily known until 1880 for his somber religious paintings, he turned, without explanation, to sculpture. Some say this resulted from his spending time in the industrial and mining regions of his country, where van Gogh was living—though the two never met—where he experienced an awakening of social consciousness. He tried painting laborers but soon found that the canvas was inadequate to express his deep feelings. The heroism of common physical exertion demanded a heroic medium—sculpture. In his native Belgium he became a leader of the avant-garde,

then began to gain recognition in France as well when he sent paintings, then sculptures, to the Paris Salon beginning in 1881. Until his death in 1905 he exhibited variations on the same topic almost every year at the salon and became an admired member of the French artistic community. In a study of Meunier's life, Christian Brinton wrote: "To have led an art from palace to factory, to have delivered her from the hands of king, priest and noble patron and presented her unfettered to the people, is not the least triumph of the nineteenth century."[42]

Jules Dalou was the first French sculptor of note to take up the theme of the contemporary worker. Next to Auguste Rodin, Dalou was France's most talented and well-known sculptor. He began his career with decorative sculpture for hotels and homes of the rich but later turned to monumental sculpture, doing only subjects that were personally important to him. We find laborers in his work as early as 1879, the year he began his monumental *Triumph of the Republic*, which took ten years to complete. Amid the monument's neobaroque and allegorical splendor, Dalou sculpted a blacksmith in contemporary dress. This was a new kind of worker, the modern workman, in his apron and sabots. His muscular body and defiant glance give the figure a forceful dignity. In the 1890s Dalou produced a model for a workers' monument that was never completed. The work exists today in a small plaster model and small figure studies. When asked about his proposed Monument to Workers, Dalou replied that such a monument was an inevitable necessity of modern times; it was "in the air."[43] By the end of the nineteenth century, the theme of labor reached such a status that not only Dalou but Rodin, the most famous sculptor of the age, designed a colossal monument to it. Unfortunately it too never progressed beyond the design stage. Rodin's *Tower of Labor* would have been more universal than anything previously conceived. The monument consisted of a tall central column topped with two large winged figures and surrounded by a spiral staircase. On the column workers were represented in relief, and as one ascended the type of labor changed from manual to mental. Rodin called it a gospel of labor. "The Middle Ages had their cathedrals," he wrote. "The soul of the populace was expressed through them, their stones were like the phrases of a canticle; they sang the enthusiasm of popular faith . . . Today, the people believe above all else in work; almost everyone puts his faith in it. Thus it is to work, to work the King, that I wish to raise a monument which would be at once architectural and sculptural."[44]

As with so many artists of that period, Young's early works were influenced by Rodin. This can be seen in general poses and figure types, but modeling of the surface shows Young's greatest debt to Rodin. A master of surface, Rodin's work came to life through his impressionistic sensitivity to the play of light. Young made at least two visits to Rodin's studio. Once when he went with an English friend, an assistant invited the young men to look around the studio and Young marvelled at the wonderful studies of arms, legs, hands, and torsos scattered throughout the room. As he studied these pieces, Rodin himself walked in:

> After looking around and nodding to us he [Rodin] proceeded to inspect and criticize the work being done. I remember very distinctly seeing him examine very attentively and very closely. It was then for the first time I realized that he was very short-sighted. After inspecting the surface with his eyes very close to the marble, he took a pencil and . . . marked some corrections and said a few words to the carver and then passed on. After he had gone

over the other works being carved, he came over and greeted us very simply and departed. Unfortunately I didn't understand French well enough to know what he said, and I don't remember my friend's translation.[45]

Young felt that the best of Rodin's works were small enough to be handled, that the greatest possible enjoyment came from feeling with one's fingers. In many ways the same can be said of Young's early statues. They are small pieces with strong emphasis on the surface modeling, and various textures and subtle light-and-shadow-play were rendered with skill to enhance the overall effect. It was Meunier and Dalou, however, rather than Rodin, who influenced Young's art directly. Not only the theme but also the poses are more like theirs than Rodin's. Young added his own unique statement, rendering laborers in classical Greek and Renaissance style with emphasis on movement and clad in contemporary apparel.

His first sculpture in Paris was a small statuette of a man with a shovel. By this time Young had become discouraged with his classes at the Académie Julian and in 1903 began to work more on his own. After obtaining some clay, he set up a stand and armature in his studio and began working on a piece he called *The Shoveler*.

His inspiration came from the streets where he observed workers and, with an image in mind one day, retired quickly to his studio and began to sculpt. As the work progressed, he returned to make sketches to better capture the pose and feeling. He relied extensively on these sketches. Whenever he went out walking he stopped and drew the workers he saw, considering this more valuable than any posed model to achieve the feeling he wanted.

The Shoveler depicts a man lifting a heavy spade of earth. The shovel handle bends and his back

Man Tired (Tired Out), 1903
BRONZE, 9″
(LOS ANGELES COUNTY MUSEUM
OF ART, MR. AND MRS. ALLAN C.
BALCH COLLECTION)

bows under the strain. Stripped to the waist, the subject clearly exposes his taut, straining muscles. The heavy, baggy trousers give the figure a contemporary and realistic feeling.

Although the workers Young saw in the streets inspired this piece, Alfred Boucher's sculpture of a man shoveling entitled *To the Earth* could have influenced Young as well. This life-sized marble was exhibited at the salon some twelve years earlier where it won critical acclaim. Afterward it became part of the Musee Galiera collection on permanent display. Young mentioned seeing it: "It was beautifully modeled and cut in marble but it didn't shovel and didn't give me the impression I perceived from the workmen, going about their jobs of removing dirt etc, from one place to another [as] I saw everywhere in the streets, so I tried a shoveler of my own."[46] Although more conservative and traditional, Boucher's classical nude has a similar pose. The difference is in Young's more honest, contemporary feeling which portrays an authentic street worker. Young saw more nobility in that than in any classical nude.

Young immediately began another work which he called *Man Tired*. Based on direct observation as before, the idea came to him while walking the narrow streets that meander off the main boulevards of Paris. There he saw a man seated on a doorstep dressed in a laborer's clothing, tired and bent over from what seemed a hard day's work. The artist made a quick sketch and went back to his studio to start another statuette, *Man Tired*.[47] The feeling of introspection and pathos in this project was unusual in Young's work, which was generally more active in feel and dynamic in pose. Seated quietly, dressed in the traditional garb of a French worker— baggy trousers, thin shirt, and brimmed hat—the worker rests on a block representing a door step,

slumped over with his head on his hand, elbows on his knees. The figure exudes a feeling of complete exhaustion; his bowed back and relaxed arms express the muscular figure of a laborer.

Man Tired shows the influence of a popular theme of the time: society's outcasts. This dominated Picasso's work of the Blue Period, though Picasso did not paint laborers. Young's close friend Eugene Higgins did. Higgins emphasized huddled, weary masses in both drawings and paintings. Two of Meunier's sculptures were also similar to *Man Tired* in theme and pose—*Miner Crouching* and *Iron Puddler*. They too emphasized the weary, exhausted laborer and provide an example of heroic-sized bronze sculptures that Young longed to do. Young saw his figures representing more than common laborers or outcasts—they were heroic and profound expressions of humanity. From the beginning he wanted these sculptures cast on a monumental scale, but at this point finances would never allow it. Young did a significant drawing during the period that reveals how he envisioned his work. The drawing, dated 1904, is of a Monument to Labor. In it the large central relief is dominated by *The Shoveler*, while *Man Tired* is positioned like Rodin's *The Thinker* in *The Gates of Hell*, which Rodin executed between 1880 and 1890. The plaster casts were first exhibited to the public in 1900. On one occasion Young said regarding Meunier's monumental sculptures: "In this quality he is outstanding among men of his day. It lies in his architectural sense of the figure; a quality Rodin was so lacking in. All Meunier's figures are larger than life no matter what their actual measurements. Few modern sculptors have had this quality and none in greater quantity than Meunier."[48]

Another of Young's works resembles Meunier. In 1904 he produced a piece called *Stevedore*,

MONUMENT TO LABOR, 1904
GRAPHITE ON PAPER, 7 1/2″ X 8″
(MSS. 4, SKETCHBOOK 28, PHOTOGRAPHIC
ARCHIVES, HAROLD B. LEE LIBRARY,
BRIGHAM YOUNG UNIVERSITY,
PROVO, UTAH)

Stevedore, 1904

BRONZE, 13 3/4″
(THE METROPOLITAN MUSEUM
OF ART, NEW YORK CITY, NEW YORK,
ROGERS FUND, 1914)

portraying a rugged dock hand leaning forward under the weight of a heavy load. The subject makes his way up a small incline, a dock plank, which Young hints at on the figure's base. The surface is roughly textured, adding to the realism and the feeling of life and animation. Of all the works Young did in Paris, *Stevedore* is most like, and seems to be inspired by, a Meunier sculpture of the same subject. (This particular work is not the best known *Stevedore* by Meunier, which was erected as a life-size statue in Belgium's port city of Antwerp. This work was of a man carrying a heavy load on his back—almost identical to Young's.)

The Shoveler and *Man Tired* brought Young delayed recognition. At first the statuettes remained in the studio without particular notice from friends or visitors. Then Young entered them in the American Art Association show in Paris in the winter of 1903. Prominent American sculptor Paul Bartlett, one of the judges, specifically singled out Young's works and spoke highly of them. Pictures of both sculptures appeared in the *Paris Herald* in a section devoted to the show. The *Herald* gave a luncheon for several of the exhibitors and included Young. Later Young sent the pieces to the Paris Salon where they were prominently displayed in the main gallery circle and again received notable mention, this time from French critics.[49]

In the midst of this success, Young's funds ran out. His uncle, John W. Young, then in Paris, offered to pay his way home if he would travel with him. So in the summer of 1903 Mahonri found himself back in Utah where he visited friends and renewed acquaintances, taking a sketching trip with Alma Wright, also just back from Paris. The two artists travelled to Cache Valley, then to Park City where they visited a school friend, Pauline Grew, and her husband, Arthur B. Davies. The

drawings in Young's sketchbooks attest to the extent of his Utah travels.[50]

At the end of a pleasant and productive summer, Young was elated to find that his mother had borrowed enough money to enable him to return to Paris. En route Young took time in New York to visit friends and catch up on trends.[51]

In Paris he immediately enrolled in an anatomy class at the Ecole des Beaux Arts. Even though he had studied anatomy with John Hafen in Salt Lake City and Kenyon Cox at the Art Students League, he still felt deficient in this area. Nevertheless his anatomy studies did not last long. In the overcrowded lecture room, the air was foul from cadavers and formaldehyde. After each class he came down with violent headaches and eventually had to drop the course.[52]

During his last two years in Paris he worked more independently than ever, sketching and drawing constantly. He continued to sculpt and completed three fine pieces—two on the theme of labor and a small statuette of his friend Alfred Maurer entitled *Alfy*. One of these works would later launch his career in America, a small statuette he called *Bovet-Arthur—A Laborer*.

One day a man named Bovet-Arthur knocked at Young's door, asking if the artist needed a model. Taken by his appearance, Young decided to hire him and the two became good friends. Engaged in long conversations as Young worked, the artist learned that Bovet-Arthur was not a typical laborer. He was born into an upper-middle class family, his father had lost his money, and Bovet-Arthur was compelled to work from early spring until late fall as a boatman on the canals. In the winter the model returned to Paris. Because work was scarce this time of year, he often frequented the Louvre and other museums to keep warm as

Bovet-Arthur— A Laborer, 1904
BRONZE, 16″
(© COURTESY MUSEUM OF ART,
BRIGHAM YOUNG UNIVERSITY.

Bovet-Arthur, 1904
CONTE ON PAPER, 10″ x 6 1/2″
(Mss.4, SKETCHBOOK 28, PHOTOGRAPHIC
ARCHIVES, HAROLD B. LEE LIBRARY,
BRIGHAM YOUNG UNIVERSITY,
PROVO, UTAH)

much as to admire the art. During breaks Young told Bovet-Arthur what he knew about art; in return, the model read to him the verses he wrote about the great masterpieces he had seen.[53]

Young began this work the morning they met, initially drawing sketches of Bovet-Arthur, then fashioning a small statuette dressed in the typical thin undershirt and baggy corduroy trousers of a Parisian workman. He posed the figure in a way that showed his dignified humility. The work took two weeks to complete. Afterward Young had the piece cast in bronze, and the next year he entered it in the Paris Salon.[54]

Bovet-Arthur's standing pose, which is proud but not pretentious, hints at a genuine respect for the man and what he stood for. Although his dress defines him as a worker, his pose is heroic. It is reminiscent of Meunier's *Stevedore* which stands strong and defiant and later became the symbol of the port city of Antwerp. A full-scale copy of this figure was displayed in the Luxembourg Palace where Young probably saw it. An over-life-sized work by Dalou, *The Great Peasant*, was completed and shown around 1900 which is similar to *Bovet-Arthur* as well in the contrapposto positioning of the body, the turn of the head, and the noble yet humble downward glance.

A short time after completing *Bovet-Arthur—A Laborer*, Young invited his friend John Gregory to see it. Gregory had criticized *The Shoveler* and *Man Tired* as unfinished, but when he saw *Bovet-Arthur* he said—not at the time but later privately—that he could no longer find fault with Young's work.[55]

The artist began another small sculpture, *The Chiseler*. As with *The Shoveler* and *Man Tired*, his inspiration came from observing working men in the streets. However, this sculpture was nude. Originally Young envisioned it in baggy trousers but for-

got to cover the clay adequately one evening and found it the next day cracked in five places. Somewhat discouraged, Young made the necessary adaptations and found that the piece turned out differently from what he had envisioned.[56]

The finished work reminds one of a Renaissance or classical piece. A muscular man crouches over a large block of stone, one knee on the block, the other foot on the ground. In one hand a chisel is held to the block, while the other holds a hammer ready to strike. The compact yet active pose is reminiscent of Myron's ancient *Discobolus*. Young admired Greek sculpture, not only for its form but for its "intense, vibrating sense of life."[57] Referring to the *Discobolus*, Young wrote:

> How does it achieve this quality [its compactness, as he called it] in such a high degree? By nothing else than by line. By line it achieves its superb unity and also its marvelous sense of movement—movement rhythmical and swift. It, in all its parts, suggests previous positions and others to follow. Nothing is static, and yet, such is the masterly use of the interplay of lines that the statue as a statue maintains a perfect equilibrium and functions perfectly within its total space.[58]

With reference to the placement of the figure on a block, as well as to the modeling and treatment of surfaces, *The Chiseler* can be compared to Rodin's *The Thinker*. With regard to the pose and subject, it is reminiscent of Dalou. This, more than any other work the artist did in Paris, had the closest affinity to the Beaux Arts style still prevalent at the time.

The Chiseler was the first of a series of laborers in the same general pose—the figure crouching over his work in the act of striking an object. Works later done in New York City that follow this theme include *The Blacksmith*, *The Farrier*, and *The Driller*, as well as *Man Sawing*. Yet his works done in Paris

Alfy (A. H. Maurer), 1904
BRONZE, 15″

are considered among his best. Nearly two decades later, in 1924 when Young was well established, an article on his laborers was illustrated with these Paris sculptures. [59]

The last piece Young did in France was a full-length portrait statuette of Alfred Maurer with whom he had become close. Young wanted to portray his friend as he had seen him so many times with hat, cape, and walking stick standing on the curb, ready to cross the street. Of all his Paris works, this is the most personal and expressive in form and surface modeling, a free interpretation of the subject rather than an exact likeness. The active and flowing surface and lack of detail give the impression of the artistic type, a sense of intrigue and mystery befitting the bohemian artist. This is the first of many of Young's portraits of artists.

As Young finished *The Chiseler* and *Alfy,* LDS apostle Heber J. Grant visited Paris on a tour of the church's French mission. A close friend of Young's parents, Grant asked him if there was anything he needed. Young said he was doing fine but wished he had the money to cast his statuettes in bronze. Grant gave him one hundred dollars. He also promised to write friends in Salt Lake City to see if they would also contribute. As a result, Young was able to cast several of his works before leaving Europe.[60]

Sensing that his time abroad was growing short, in 1905 Young decided to make a final trip to Italy. He considered Italy "the mother of art" and regretted that his first trip had been short. This time he scheduled a four-month itinerary. He visited Genoa, Pisa, Rome, Florence, and Padua, always sketching and painting. He felt that this was an ideal finale to his time in Europe.

Later, when Young was teaching at the Art Students League, the American artist Rockwell Kent

asked if he recommended studying in Europe. In a letter, Young advised him to get the fundamentals in the United States and then study in Europe, as he had done. In his journal he wrote:

The last two years abroad were the most valuable. During them, something of the ten years of struggle and study began to take form and fairly definite conclusions were reached. I had been to London several times and I knew pretty

The Chiseler, 1903-04,
BRONZE, 9 1/2″

thoroughly what was in Paris, but a second trip to Italy was like adding up a long line of figures. How clearly I remembered a saying of Sargent's that one needed ten years of study. In the impatience of youth how ridiculous that seemed; years were so long and contained such infinite possibilities. I remembered Salt Lake too, and our doctor, Harry B. Niles saying, "Study until you are forty, and you'll know more than anybody in the world." I knew I had much still to learn but I felt I had laid down a fairly solid foundation.[61]

Concerning American artists who studied abroad during this period, Milton Brown wrote, "The majority collected a particular bag of tricks,

Laborers, CA. 1912
GRAPHITE ON PAPER, 4″ X 5 3/4″
(MSS. 4, SKETCHBOOK 19,
PHOTOGRAPHIC ARCHIVES,
HAROLD B. LEE LIBRARY
BRIGHAM YOUNG UNIVERSITY,
PROVO, UTAH)

assumed the artist's mien, and returned to a culture which had suddenly become unreceptive."[62] This may have been true of many artists who returned disappointed to their homeland, but for Young his education in Paris was more than a bag of tricks. In Paris he came into his own. Later in life he was asked how he accounted for his success as a student:

> They [other students] were just learning one thing . . . I could do what they were doing in Salt Lake or New York, if I could get a model, but I couldn't go to the Louvre. . . . I was trying to get as broad a base as possible on which to grow. That's why I worked at everything and took time to go to all the museums and a great deal of exhibitions. I had long made up my mind not to loaf in my studio. If I wasn't working I went out and if I did nothing else I just watched the passing show. And I'm not so sure I could have done better.[63]

Notes

1. *The Kennedy Galleries Are Host to the Hundredth Anniversary Exhibition of Paintings and Sculptures by 100 Artists Associated with The Art Students League of New York, Exhibition Catalogue* (New York: The Art Students League and the Kennedy Galleries, 1975), 15-24.

2. Mahonri M. Young, "Notes at the Beginning," in *Mahonri M. Young: Retrospective Exhibition* (Andover, MA: Addison Gallery of American Art, 1940), 51.

3. Mahonri M. Young, "Miscellaneous (as filed by Mahonri M. Young: continued)," Mahonri M. Young Collection, Mss. 4, box 6, folder 38, Archives and Manuscripts, Brigham Young University, Provo, Utah.

4. Ibid.

5. Young, "Etching," box 5, folder 51.

6. Young, "Miscellaneous (as filed by Mahonri M. Young: continued)."

7. Young, "Cox, Kenyon," box 5, folder 33.

8. Young, "Miscellaneous (as filed by Mahonri M. Young: continued)."

9. Ibid.

10. Kenyon Cox, *The Classic Point of View* (New York: W. W. Norton Co., 1980), xlix-lv.

11. Young, "Heavy Sledge and Man with a Pick," box 6, folder 6.

12. Walt and Roger Reed, *The Illustrator in America, 1880-1980: A Century of Illustration* (New York: Madison Square Press, Inc., 1984), 31.

13. Young, "Miscellaneous (as filed by Mahonri M. Young: continued)."

14. Young, "Notes at the Beginning," box 6, folder 42.

15. Young, "The Salt Lake Tribune," box 7, folder 10.

16. Young, "Miscellaneous (as filed by Mahonri M. Young: continued)."

17. Patricia J. Pierce, *The Ten* (Hingham, MA: Pierce Galleries, Inc., 1976), 9.

18. Young, "Richards, Lee Greene," box 7, folder 5.

19. Young, "Eighteeneth Ward Square," box 5, folder 49.

20. Young, "Notes at the Beginning."

21. Ibid.

22. Young, "Boston to Liverpool," box 5, folder 15.

23. Young, "Richards, Lee Greene."

24. Young, "Barnard, George Grey," box 5, folder 8.

25. Young, "Julian Academy, 1901-2; Jean-Paul Laurens' class," box 6, folder 18.

26. Young, "Notes at the Beginning," *Mahonri M. Young: Retrospective Exhibition*, 51.

27. Young, "Miscellaneous (as filed by Mahonri M. Young: continued.)"

28. Young, "Glackens, William J.," box 5, folder 63.

29. Milton W. Brown, *American Painting From the Armory Show to the Depression* (Princeton, NJ: Princeton University Press, 1972), 28-31.

30. Young, "Notes at the Beginning."

31. Elizabeth McCausland, *A. H. Maurer* (New York: A. A. Wyn, Inc., for the Walker Art Center, 1951), 71, 237.

32. Young, "Paris, 1901-1905, 1923-1925," box 6, folder 45.

33. Young, "Millet, J. F.," box 6, folder 35.

34. Young, "Etching."

35. Young, "Notes at the Beginning," *Mahonri M. Young: Retrospective Exhibition*, 53.

36. Young, "Notes at the Beginning."

37. "Town Builders of Today," *Survey* 52 (1 July 1924): 393.

38. Ibid. The Pioneers knew that settling the Valley of the Great Salt Lake could only be achieved through hard work. The first pioneers making their way to the area met Jim Bridger, who was reported to have said he would give one thousand dollars for the first bushel of corn raised in the valley. Although this statement was probably never made, it became a popular saying in Mormon lore, a symbol that with God's help and hard work they could beat the odds. In his journal Brigham Young wrote "[the valley is] a place where a good living will require hard labor," but it would "be coveted by no other people" (Leonard J. Arrington, *Great Basin Kingdom: Economic History of the Latter-day Saints* [Lincoln: University of Nebraska Press, 1958], 41). Hard work was preached from the pulpit and practiced in daily life. Consider the sermon delivered by Brigham Young from the tabernacle in June 1873:

> Follow the spirit of improvement and labor. All the capital there is upon the earth is the bone and sinew of working men and women. . . . Labor builds our meeting houses, temples, court houses, fine halls for music and fine school houses; it is labor that teaches our children, and makes them acquainted with the various branches of education, that makes them proficient in their own language and in other languages understood by the children of men; and all this enhances the wealth and the glory and the comfort of any people on the earth (*Journal of Discourses*, 16 [Liverpool, 1874]: 66).

39. See Wayne Craven, *American Art: History on Culture* (Madison, WI: Brown and Benchmark, 1994), 330.

40. John M. Hunisak, "Images of Workers: From Genre Treatment and Heroic Nudity to the Monument to Labor," in Peter Fusco and H. W. Janson, *The Romantics to Rodin, French Nineteenth-Century Sculpture for North American Collections* (Los Angeles: Los Angeles County Museum of Art, 1980), 52.

41. Boucher's piece is illustrated in ibid., 53.

42. Frank Owen Payne, "The Tribute of American Sculpture to Labor," *Art and Archaeology* 6 (Aug. 1917): 83.

43. Hunisak in Fusco and Janson, 59. Today Dalou is considered the most significant sculptor of contemporary labor in nineteenth-century France.

44. Ibid.

45. Young, "Rodin, Auguste," box 7, folder 7.

46. Young, "Gregory, John," box 6, folder 1.

47. Ibid.

48. Young, "Millet, J. F."

49. Young, "Gregory, John."

50. Young, "Trip Home, 1903 and 1905," box 7, folder 18.

51. Ibid.

52. Young, "Julian Academy, 1901-2; Jean-Paul Laurens' Class."

53. Young, "Bovet-Arthur— A Laborer," box 5, folder 16.

54. Ibid.

55. Young, "Gregory, John."

56. Ibid.

57. Young, "Mahonri Young to Mss. Mannes, April 10, 1928," box 3.

58. Ibid.

59. "Town Builders of Today."

60. Young, "Paris, 1901-1905, 1923-1925."

61. Young, "Notes at the Beginning," *Mahonri M. Young: Retrospective Exhibition*, 56.

62. Milton W. Brown et al., *American Art: Painting, Sculpture, Architecture, Decorative Arts, Photography* (New York: Prentice Hall, Inc., Harry N. Abrams, 1979), 488.

63. Young, "Gregory, John."

CHAPTER FIVE.

Years of Struggle: Salt Lake City

I look back on those years as my years of exile.
Life was to me on grimmest terms. Studying art and life was no longer the main concern.

—Mahonri Young

Mahonri Young returned from Paris during the second half of 1905 with great hopes and expectations. Secure in his academic training, he was eager to find opportunities to prove himself. He knew full well that Salt Lake City was not Paris, but he assumed that Utahns would want to improve their cultural surroundings.

In the United States in general sculpture was conservative. American statues still languished in the tradition of the past century, with little change since the Civil War. The influence of neoclassicism held sway. In 1856 Erastus Dow Palmer expressed the role of American statuary in terms that still held credence as the twentieth century began:

> The mission of the sculptor's art is not to imitate forms alone, but through them to reveal the purest and best of our nature. And no work of sculpture however well wrought out physically, results in excellence unless it rests upon, and is sustained by the dignity of a moral or intellectual intuition.[1]

America's most famous and respected sculptors exemplified these ideals—Augustus Saint-Gaudens and Daniel Chester French, whose influence and work dominated sculpture during the last quarter of the nineteenth century and well into the next. Even as late as the 1930s, having been a pupil or assistant of Saint-Gaudens or French was often a deciding factor in gaining a public commission.[2] Both artists were trained at the Ecole des Beaux Arts, and their work shows the influence of the classical academic tradition combined with a new awareness of Renaissance and Baroque sculpture. With these influences, they translated American themes into idealized symbols. Representative of their work was French's *Alma Mater* (Columbia University, 1903), and Saint-Gaudens's Admiral Farragut Monument (New York City, 1881), and the Adams Memorial (Washington, D.C., 1891).

Another influence began to be felt in America at the turn of the twentieth century: the growing fame and importance of Auguste Rodin. Among the first American sculptors to be influenced by him were Lorado Taft and George Grey Barnard, who extolled the artist's style throughout this country. Barnard spent twelve years in Paris. His *Struggle of the Two Natures of Man* combines Rodin's vigorously-modeled surfaces and Michelangelo's expressive action and intense emotion. Barnard was one of the most innovative and original sculptors of his time in America. Rodin's influence shifted tastes toward greater naturalism, which can be seen in the work of Paul Weyland Bartlett. In his *Democracy Protecting the Arts of Peace,* commissioned for the United States House of Representatives, Bartlett blended this new-found naturalism with late nineteenth-century French and American decorative qualities.

Even so these artists were the exception rather than the rule. Styles and trends slowly changed, as public commissions remained an essential part of a sculptor's success. Until modern sculpture took hold in America, the art of sculpture was inseparably connected with patronage. Unlike painting, which tolerated individual eccentricities, sculpture was a public art. Conservatism can be seen even in mid-century public works by Joseph Colletti and others, and even up to Frederick Hart's recent sculptural addition to the Vietnam War Memorial in Washington, D.C.

Upon Young's return, Utah was on the eve of a period of great change, which heightened the artist's sense that he would play an important role. The Mormon church had just passed through one of its hardest periods following years of persecution as a result of the Edmunds-Tucker Act. Enmeshed in the polygamy problem as the nineteenth century closed, Utahns in general and the church in particular strove for acceptance as part of mainstream America. As Cyrus Dallin before him, Mahonri Young saw in the Latter-day Saint church the potential for commissions commemorating church

and state history and celebrating famous leaders. But Young soon found this avenue for patronage frustrating.

Although Young had worked hard as a student, he found it even harder to establish himself as a professional artist. The next five years, from 1905 to 1910, were "years of worry, struggle, and discouragement": "There was no time or need to study life—its facts were too immediate; everywhere they stared me in the face; they could not be ignored or side stepped. When forced to, we generally find the strength."[3]

Ever-present financial worries compounded his artistic struggle. He still owed his family for his studies in Paris, so he conserved money by living temporarily with his mother at 174 C Street. However, earnings from a few small commissions and the art lessons he taught soon allowed him to rent an apartment and set up his own studio.

His first commission, and without a doubt the most unusual of his career, came shortly after his arrival home. One day in September a man from the Frost Creamery came to the door and asked the artist if he would be interested in carving a figure in butter for the company's exhibit at the Utah State Fair that month for twenty-five dollars. The day before the fair opened, Young took his sculpting tools to the fairgrounds where he began work on a three-foot-high block in a refrigerated glass case. *The Dairy Maid,* as she was called, started to take form. Young worked with the case door open until the butter became too soft to work, then he closed the door until it hardened again. After finishing, Young toured the other exhibits. A short time later a young employee of the Frost Creamery came running up exclaiming, "The girl is melting!" Young returned to find that someone had left the door open. The dairy maid's head was on her

Scrubwoman, 1908
PLASTER, 8″
(PHOTOGRAPHIC ARCHIVES,
HAROLD B. LEE LIBRARY,
BRIGHAM YOUNG UNIVERSITY,
PROVO, UTAH)

breast. He resculpted her, afterward instructing workers to keep the door closed.[4]

With the money he earned from this and other small commissions, Young opened an art class of twelve students at the YMCA building. The class was short-lived, however, for one of the older students, Bill Curtis, organized an art club that eventually took most of the students. Deeply hurt, Young continued to give private lessons and rented a studio on the fifth floor of the Hooper building in downtown Salt Lake City.[5] Moving his studio resulted in an unexpected commission. The Ware Traganza Architectural Firm occupied the same building. Traganza proposed that Young paint a mural for the new Isis Theater under construction, with the stipulation that it had to be completed within a month. Young would need help to meet this deadline, so he asked Lee Richards, who was without work at the time, to assist him. Richards

Reading the Headlines, 1910

readily agreed. The project became a cooperative effort. Young did the design and Richards, a painter, sketched it. The main motif consisted of large masks of Comedy and Tragedy. Unable to afford models, each artist posed for the other. The successful completion ahead of schedule pleased the firm.[6]

During those early years Young was often without work. Finding it a challenge to keep himself busy, he often went to his favorite spot, Godbe Pitts Drugstore[7] on the corner of First South and Main Street. Here the trolley lines intersected from all over town. People waited at the corner for the trolley car that was drawn by small Mexican mules. Young sketched the workers: icemen making deliveries, butchers, bums, men and women drinking in bars, scrubwomen, peddlers, loggers. Any activity caught his attention, particularly those of the workers. Young believed that "The worker is the essential man."[8]

Although there are numerous drawings of workers from this period, sculptures are almost nonexistent. In Salt Lake City the artist did not continue the theme he had focused on in Paris. The exception is a small statuette called *Scrubwoman*. This work depicts the most menial of labor. The figure is on her hands and knees scrubbing the floor. The handling of the surface is free and expressive with no attention given to the detail of the figure. She is just another subject of honest toil. Focusing on the labor she performs and on her strength and dignity, Young does not seem to intentionally moralize or make social comment. She is not pretty or dainty. She works as hard as any man. Young's women are real people who do real work. There is nothing idealized or romanticized about them.

People he saw at the corner became the inspiration for two small statuettes, *The Halt and the Blind* and *Reading the Headlines*. The former was based on a ritual that seemed to occur daily: each day a tall blind man and a much shorter newspaperman who had lost one leg just below the hip met at a post diagonally across the corner from the drugstore. The newspaperman read to his blind friend. The latter was of a newspaperman and a friend.[9] Both of these works, meant to be viewed from the front, seem to have a narrative quality about them. Considering these to be experiments in impressionist sculpture, Young wrote that he intended to suggest the feeling of a cold misty evening in late fall. More than any other works he did during this time, they tend to have a narrative and anecdotal quality that were the sculptural equivalent of the Ashcan paintings dealing with the common, unglamorized side of American neighborhoods. During this time, Young also painted several small canvases in subject and style reminiscent of Ashcan realism. Starting his career in an artistic milieu dominated by nineteenth-century traditions and ideals—a combination of French academic style, Beaux Arts training, the newly-found tendency toward naturalism, and the Rodinesque handling of the surface—these works had very little marketable value. Though based on characters he knew in Salt Lake City, the works are dated 1910 and most likely done soon after his arrival in New York City.

During this period Young sculpted his first work dealing with a western theme.[10] By the turn of the century western sculpture had become popular due to the work of such artists as Cyrus Dallin and Frederic Remington. Young hoped he would have success with this subject, too. His statue *The Prospector* depicts a miner leading his packed burrow. The textured modeling of the surface gives an added sense of ruggedness. It did not prove to be immediately successful, but the work was later bought by the Rio Grande Railroad and used on the insignia for some specially-manufactured rail cars named *The Prospector*.[11]

Hoping to attract patronage during his first year home, Young turned to portraiture. One of the first, a portrait bust of B. H. Roberts, a prominent Mormon church leader and writer, was intended to draw attention. Young felt that if it was well received, it would bring favorable publicity as well as badly needed financial assistance. Roberts consented to pose for the artist. For financial reasons, the clay bust was not cast until 1908 when it was sent to Chicago along with Young's later statues of Joseph and Hyrum Smith. Nor did the Roberts portrait prove to be financially rewarding. Although it was generally well received, the Roberts family declined purchase. Roberts's wife did not like it, saying that it did not show the "sweetness" of her husband.[12] In 1936 Young sold the bust to a daughter of B. H. Roberts for the price it had cost him to have it cast.[13]

In 1906 Young won some local prizes. A small bust received the prize for sculpture at the Utah State Fair, and a painting, *The Blacksmith*, garnered a three-hundred-dollar award at the Utah Art Institute show. What furthered his reputation the most at this time was a bust of Alfred Lambourne, a prominent local poet and painter to whom Young was introduced. Lambourne was best known for romantic realist landscapes. With much in common, Young and Lambourne became close friends. Young prevailed upon Lambourne to pose for him and proceeded to do several drawings as well as a portrait bust. When done, it was first exhibited at the national academy of design and then in Utah. Sold at a profit, the *Alfred Lambourne* bust was well received and is now part of the permanent collection of the State of Utah.[14]

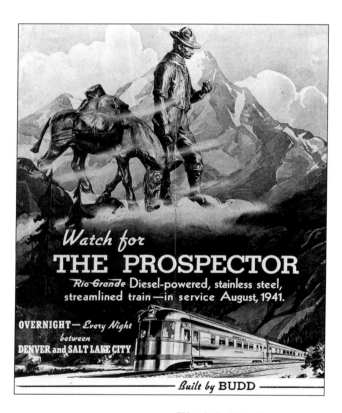

Watch for The Prospector

(Photographic Archives, Harold B. Lee Library, Brigham Young University, Provo Utah)

Both the Roberts and Lambourne busts are excellent examples of Young's early portrait style, which show a strong influence from Rodin. In Young's opinion, Rodin was a master of portraiture, and in his writings he particularly praised his bust of Jean-Paul Laurens for its power of execution and strong likeness: "It is superb in its solid modeling and grand in its composition and design. It is also completely finished; there are no raw edges or unexplained surfaces. The treatment of the hair and beard are fine in character and texture with a fine decorative treatment which takes nothing away from the reality."[15] The *B. H. Roberts* bust, the more conservative of the two, shows less Rodinesque surface texture. The *Alfred Lambourne* bust, however, shows the French master's influence in psychological expression as well as in the even stronger surface modeling.

Soon after returning to Salt Lake City, Young induced Lee Richards to take him to meet a young woman he had seen in Salt Lake City before studying in Paris, and had seen again in Paris in 1904 where she was studying music. Cecelia's father, James Sharp, had lost his fortune and Cecelia had to discontinue her study of piano to return home. Young had been visiting the Heber John family in Paris when Cecelia came by with her friend, Louise Richards, to tell the John family goodbye. Although they were not introduced, Mahonri was determined to meet her one day.[16]

After meeting her in her music studio, Mahonri courted Cecelia despite his financial circumstances and her older age. She was five years his senior. Before long the couple decided to marry.

The Prospector, 1907
BRONZE, 26″
(PHOTOGRAPHIC ARCHIVES,
HAROLD B. LEE LIBRARY,
BRIGHAM YOUNG UNIVERSITY,
PROVO, UTAH)

B. H. Roberts, 1906-09

BRONZE, 23″
(PHOTOGRAPHIC ARCHIVES,
HAROLD B. LEE LIBRARY,
BRIGHAM YOUNG UNVIERSITY,
PROVO, UTAH)

Alfred Lambourne, 1907-09
PLASTER, 18″
(PHOTOGRAPHIC ARCHIVES,
HAROLD B. LEE LIBRARY,
BRIGHAM YOUNG UNIVERSITY,
PROVO, UTAH)

CECELIA SHARP, CA. 1906
(PHOTOGRAPHIC ARCHIVES, HAROLD B. LEE LIBRARY,
BRIGHAM YOUNG UNIVERSITY, PROVO, UTAH)

MAHONRI YOUNG, CA. 1906
(PHOTOGRAPHIC ARCHIVES,
LEE LIBRARY)

One of the most beautiful and sensitive of Young's portraits was the bust he did of Cecelia. Here he portrayed in an elegant and sensitive way some of the feeling he had for her delicacy and femininity as well as his love for her. This work was undoubtedly influenced in concept and style by the Italian portrait busts of the Quattrocento. Young's sculpture of Cecelia in particular, with this subtle and delicate modeling, reminds one of the work of Desiderio da Settignano.

After the favorable reception of the Lambourne bust, Young decided to approach the Mormon church about the possibility of doing a life-sized statue of church founder Joseph Smith, Jr., using the Roberts and the Lambourne busts as evidence of his ability. Young was aware that the church had in its possession the death mask of Smith, which he proposed to use as an aid in modeling the facial features. His proposal was well received, but instead of granting Young a commission they decided to allow him to use the death mask to model a clay bust, after which a final decision would be made. In March the plaster-cast death mask was turned over to Young by church president Joseph F. Smith, grandnephew of Joseph Smith, with the stipulation that it be kept at all times in a safety vault when not in use. Hoping to secure the $4,800 commission, Young soon completed "a very good likeness," but the church hesitated to make a decision. Construction was underway on the Hotel Utah, which limited available funds.

Unemployed, approaching marriage, and desperately in need of money, Young took a job as a ranch hand for the summer at the Clayton Ranch in East Canyon, bringing with him his sketchbook to record the labors of ranch life. But Young was pleasantly surprised when in January 1907 church authorities authorized President Smith to negotiate with Young for a life-sized statue of Joseph Smith, a commission on "which my future success largely depends," Young noted.[17]

Meanwhile, on 19 February 1907 Cecelia and Mahonri married. The couple lived with the bride's parents for a few months. Then in Young's "greatest hour of need" President Smith agreed to have him cast the Joseph Smith, Jr. statue, advancing him $150 a month for a twelve-month period during which he was expected to complete the project.[18]

The Youngs moved into their own quarters, but unable to find a suitable studio in Salt Lake City, Mahonri used his own dining room to sculpt the plaster cast. Young worked that year under extremely adverse circumstances, which he felt affected the quality of his work. Among other things, he found the clay and plaster and other equipment available in Utah unsatisfactory. When the statue was completed, it was rejected.

Cecelia was expecting their first child. In desperation Young offered to do another statue of Joseph Smith at no additional cost if the church would commission a companion piece of Joseph Smith's older brother, Hyrum, father of President Joseph F. Smith. This he offered to do for $4,500. The church accepted his proposal, insisting that the modeling be done under close supervision. Young was provided with a studio in the church's Social Hall Building in downtown Salt Lake City which he found satisfactory after it was equipped with a skylight. The work went much better. When

Cecelia Sharp, 1906
PLASTER, 23"
(PHOTOGRAPHIC ARCHIVES,
HAROLD B. LEE LIBRARY,
BRIGHAM YOUNG UNIVERSITY,
PROVO, UTAH)

finished, the statues were shipped to Chicago, along with the Roberts bust, for casting, after which they occupied niches on either side of the main door of the Salt Lake temple. Later they were moved to pedestals on Temple Square where they have remained to the present day.[19]

In these works, emphasis is on historical accuracy rather than artistic expression. In all aspects of this commission, Young's work was closely overseen by the church. He used the death masks of the two men to ensure an accurate likeness and had at his disposal an old painting showing both Joseph and Hyrum in profile. This was said to be the only known original work to show both men full length.[20] Comparing the painting with the sculptures, it seems likely that the painting was the source of the clothing worn by the two men, including the walking stick in the *Hyrum Smith* statue. *Joseph Smith* holds a book representing the Book of Mormon.

Because the statues were designed for the two niches by the main doors of the Salt Lake temple, their present location does not show them to their best advantage nor does it do justice to the artist's original intent. The poses are rigid, obviously meant to be seen from the front. Their heads are turned, Joseph to his left, Hyrum to his right, resulting from the fact that the niches are recessed, one on each side of the two doors. The figures are meant to look out from their respective positions.

With the success of the Joseph and Hyrum Smith statues, Young sought other commissions

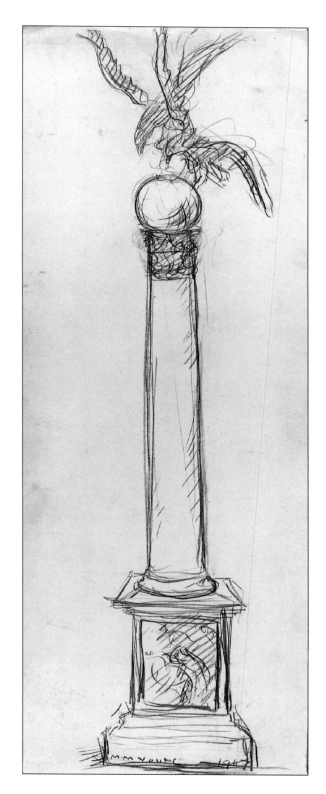

OPPOSITE:

Joseph Smith AND **Hyrum Smith**, 1907-08
BRONZE, LIFE-SIZE
TEMPLE SQUARE, SALT LAKE CITY, UTAH
PHOTO BY CRAIG LAW

SEA GULL MONUMENT, 1907
CHARCOAL ON PAPER, 11″ x 9″

Field Day, 1909
(DESERET GYMNASIUM FRIEZE)

CONCRETE, 4′ X 50′, DESTROYED
(SEE BUILDING FRONT BELOW)
(PHOTOGRAPHIC ARCHIVES,
HAROLD B. LEE LIBRARY,
BRIGHAM YOUNG UNIVERSITY,
PROVO, UTAH)

DESERET GYMNASIUM FRONT, WITH FRIEZE
DETAIL ABOVE

from the church. In 1907 he presented the idea of the Sea Gull Monument to commemorate an important chapter of Mormon pioneer history. The idea came to Young late in 1907 when George Carpenter asked him to do some sea gull drawings for the Christmas edition of the *Deseret News*. Soon thereafter he presented his proposal to commemorate the "miracle of the gulls."

Mormon pioneers had depended on a successful harvest in 1848. Even after frosts and drought, they still expected a reasonable yield on the five thousand acres they had planted until crickets invaded their crops. The settlers did everything they could to stop them. Trenches were dug around the fields and filled with water in hopes of stopping the pests; they drove them into fires; they beat them back with clubs, brooms, and other implements, all to no avail. Just when all seemed lost, thousands of sea gulls arrived and began feasting on the crickets, saving enough of the crops to support the settlers through the coming winter. This became a symbol of God's mercy to the pioneers.[21]

Church leaders were excited about Young's proposal. But although the idea was enthusiastically received, no funds were available. To Young's dismay, the project had to be postponed.

Failing to secure this commission, Young turned his attention to another project that had already been approved. The design of the Deseret Gymnasium, which was under construction, called for fifty feet of sculpted relief between three to

four feet high, cast in concrete, showing figures engaged in athletic events. The commission would
award the artist $2,000.[22] When the contract giving
Mahonri the job was presented to Willard Young,
Mahonri's uncle, who was head of the LDS school,
he declined to sign, wishing to avoid charges of
nepotism. Undaunted Mahonri obtained his uncle's signature with the aid of Willard's assistant.
The contract was placed in the middle of a stack
of papers on the assumption that Young would sign
them without reading them. When he discovered
the deception, Willard was furious. He threatened
to inform church leaders of this until it was

Hotel Utah Construction Sight, 1909
GRAPHITE ON PAPER, 5 1/2″ X 7″
(MSS. 4, SKETCHBOOK 4,
PHOTOGRAPHIC ARCHIVES,
HAROLD B. LEE LIBRARY,
BRIGHAM YOUNG UNIVERSITY,
PROVO, UTAH)

pointed out how bad it would look that he signed contracts without reading them.[23]

Mahonri set up his studio in two large adjoining rooms in the Templeton Building across the street from the new gymnasium and hired his cousin, Lawrence Thatcher, as a model. When Thatcher left to attend school, Young hired Alonzo Lewis. The frieze depicting an athletic field day was divided into three parts, a long panel flanked by two shorter ones above the main entrance to the building. The long central panel depicts participants in field events: a pole-vaulter, shot-putter, hurdlers, and a hammer-thrower. A foot race is depicted on either side: the left represents the start, the right the sprint for the finish line. The total effect is similar to the Parthenon frieze. Young created an overall movement and rhythm by how he placed and grouped the figures as they move across the façade. Two more friezes on the ends of the building each bore the monogram LDS, representing the official name of the church, along with the figures of two athletes.

Because this commission did not deal with church-related subject matter, Young's work was not overseen as rigorously as had been the case

with the *Joseph Smith* and *Hyrum Smith* statues. Although work in general went well, the project did not proceed without complications. Sculpting the commission for $2,000, Young felt he was already underpaid. Adding insult to injury, the artist was unable to complete the sculpture to his own satisfaction. He worked carefully believing that an artist could be forgiven for being late but not for bad work. Willard Young, who felt his nephew was not fast enough, had the construction crew remove the scaffold without consulting the artist first. One figure was left uncompleted.[24]

Disappointed with how the gymnasium project had gone, as well as his failure to secure a contract for the Sea Gull Monument, Young felt he would do better in New York City. In Salt Lake City he had tested the water. His quest to gain commissions and patronage from the LDS church had proved to be difficult. He had experimented with western themes with *The Prospector* and with realism with *Scrubwoman*. In order to realize his professional goals, he knew he would have to move. In New York there was more stimulus and greater opportunities. It was a place where the art world would also be more accepting of his realistic style.

Notes

1. Quoted in Tom Armstrong et al., *200 Years of American Sculpture* (New York: Whitney Museum of American Art, 1976), 114.

2. Ibid., 117.

3. Mahonri M. Young, "Notes at the Beginning," Mahonri Young Collection, Mss. 4, box 6, folder 42, Archives and Manuscripts, Harold B. Lee Library, Brigham Young University, Provo, Utah.

4. Young, "The Block," box 5, folder 12.

5. Young, "The Class—1905," box 5, folder 29.

6. Young, "The Isis," box 6, folder 13.

7. Young, "Godbe Pitts Corner," box 5, folder 65.

8. Young, "Notes at the Beginning."

9. Ibid.

10. He had an obvious affinity for this subject, for even during these years, when he was unemployed and soon to be married, he took a job as a ranch hand at the Clayton Ranch in East Canyon.

11. In 1941 the Rio Grande Railroad ordered from the Edward G. Budd Manufacturing Company two stainless steel diesel-electric rail motor car units of two cars each for overnight service between Denver and Salt Lake City via the Moffat Tunnel route. The two units of train No. 1 were named *John Evans* and *David Moffat*; those of No. 2, *Brigham Young* and *Heber C. Kimball*. About this, Beebe and Clegg comment, "Thus evenly dividing the honors between the Mormon saints to the west and Colorado gentiles to the east. The little trains were given the name *The Prospectors* and Mahonri Young's sculpture was used for the trains' insignia." See Lucius Beebe and Charles Clegg, *Rio Grande: Mainline of the Rockies* (Berkeley, CA: Howell-North, 1962), 348-51.

12. Young, "Roberts, B. H.," box 7, folder 6.

13. Ibid.

14. Young, "Lambourne, Alfred," box 6, folder 21.

15. Young, "Rodin, Auguste," box 7, folder 7.

16. Young, "Paris, 1901-1905, 1923-1925," box 6, folder 45.

17. Wayne Kendall Hinton, "A Biographical History of Mahonri M. Young, a Western American Artist," Ph.d. diss., Brigham Young University, 1974, 112.

18. Ibid.

19. Young, "Notes at the Beginning."

20. Wilford C. Wood, *Joseph Smith Begins His Work* (Salt Lake City: Deseret News Press, 1958), illustration and affidavit, unnumbered page. Prints based on this painting were popular and well known in Utah at that time.

21. For the traditional account, see Joseph Fielding Smith, *Essentials of Church History* (Salt Lake City: Deseret Book Co., 1971), 384-85.

22. Young, "L.D.S. Gymnasium Frieze," box 6, folder 22.

23. Ibid.

24. Ibid.

CHAPTER SIX.

Early Success:
New York City and Leonia, New Jersey

My sensation was that of a man on a steep roof. . . .
But at last the slipping stopped and I started to climb back.

—Mahonri Young

Resolved to escape the "worry, struggle and discouragement" he had experienced in Salt Lake City, Young began what he called his "siege of New York."[1] During his struggle in Utah, he had kept in contact with the New York art scene, making visits in 1908 and 1909. He knew that the artistic environment there would provide him with greater opportunities as well as with colleagues and patrons more sympathetic to his work. Well aware of the growing realist movement championed by Robert Henri and the Group of Eight, Young was convinced that his career would advance more rapidly in the progressive atmosphere of the East.

Three major developments occurred during this period. First, he returned to the theme of labor in sculpture; second, the Mormon church gave him the go-ahead on the Sea Gull Monument; and, third, he received a series of commissions from the American Museum of Natural History. These three

projects occupied him, often simultaneously, throughout the decade. Here each will be covered separately.

In 1910 the Youngs moved to New York City despite financial struggles. Upon their arrival they rented a temporary studio in the Old Miller Building on 65th Street and Broadway, where they also lived. Young quickly struck up friendships with other New York artists. The realist painter Leon Kroll, who had his studio in the same building, introduced Young to Paul Dougherty, a painter of marine scenes and landscapes. Mahonri also became friends with Gifford Beal and Bryson Burroughs. After a short time, the Youngs moved to more accommodating quarters on 80th Street and Broadway, which became the family's home and the artist's studio for the next two years.[2]

Given Mahonri's friendly nature, the Young home soon became a gathering place for other artists, especially those from Utah. His hospitality intensified the family's financial predicament when some of his protégés began to make his studio their home. The first of these, Hal Burrows, came from Utah to study at the Art Students League with Robert Henri and Walt Kuhn. He not only stayed at Young's studio without paying rent but received free art instruction from Young as well. Unknown to Young, Burrows invited a friend to move in with him. After putting up with this for several months, and arriving home one day after one of Burrows's parties to find the place a mess, he asked the two to move out. Burrows went on to become a successful painter, illustrator, and the art director of Metro-Goldwyn-Mayer Studios in Hollywood from 1922 to 1958.

A short time later, Young's boyhood friend, John Held, Jr., arrived from Salt Lake City so bewildered by New York that Young invited him to move into the studio. Learning that Held was married and had left his wife in Utah, Young sent for her. She too had a hard time adjusting to the big city and became so homesick that she managed to make life miserable for everyone. To occupy her, Held had his wife go out and sell some of his paintings. She gave her customers the impression that she was the artist. By the end of the day, she had sold them all, with orders for more. Soon Myrtle Held had a reputation as a "lady illustrator." Her fame grew and *Vanity Fair* featured her in an article which led to contracts to supply work for *Vanity Fair* and *Vogue* magazines. With the success of the "Myrtle Helds," the couple moved to their own apartment. Myrtle's career as an illustrator, however, was short-lived. During World War I, John was called into the army and the drawings suddenly ceased. When John returned from Europe, the couple divorced, which brought an end to the mysteriously short career of Myrtle Held.

Having taught her in one of his art classes, Young could testify that Myrtle had not done the illustrations. In Young's words, she had absolutely no talent.[3] John, however, went on to become famous in the history of American illustration, and in the 1920s his Flapper Girl illustrations became the icon of the era that replaced the Gibson Girl as the image of the American female.

Young's circle of friends by this time included many of New York City's better-known artists, among them Burroughs, Beal, Kroll, and Dougherty, who lived in a luxurious studio-apartment on West 67th Street. When the Youngs moved back to 65th Street, only a short distance from Dougherty's studio, the two became close. These artists formed an informal group that spent hours discussing art and working together. Joining with several former Salt Lake City artists including Hal Burrows, John Held, Lawrence Squires, Waldo Park Midgley, and Charles Downing, they held life drawing sessions at Young's studio at 5:00 p.m. each evening to improve their figure-drawing skills.[4] Young loved to eat out and organized a dinner club of artists and friends. The group's only rule was that no women were allowed. They met weekly at a favorite Chinese restaurant in Chinatown. The group became known as the "Hon Young Tong" and met regularly from 1913 to 1923.[5]

During the first two years in New York the Youngs fought a constant battle to make ends meet. Although Mahonri's friends were a great support to him, this was one of the most trying times of his career. He later wrote: "[I was] always slipping, only able, at the best, to delay the hideous downward progress, no matter how hard my fingers were driven in. At best it was only a delay and never a recovery—and always in sight the yawning gulf."[6]

In 1911 a son was born. Following the family

tradition established by Young's parents, they named the child Mahonri Sharp Young. Because their family was growing and the children were getting older, the Youngs decided to move out of the city in 1914 to Leonia, New Jersey. The town had a reputation as an artist's colony and had attracted a number of well-known contemporary illustrators. Among those who lived and worked in this rural setting were Harry Wickey, Grant Reynard, Dean Cornwall, and Frank Street. In 1915 Harvey Dunn and Charles Chapman would start the Leonia School of Illustration.

Young first became acquainted with Leonia through his Paris roommate Howard McCormick who lived there. McCormick introduced Young to his nephew Peter Newell, a well-known author and illustrator of children's books who also lived and worked in Leonia. In 1912 Young sculpted Newell's portrait and two years later became his neighbor when his family took up residence at 148 Prospect Street. Mahonri found the more rural environment to his liking, as his delightful etching *First Snow at Leonia* attests. Leonia became the source of many drawings and paintings during this period.

While living in Leonia, Young was often visited by his friends who had originally lived in Salt Lake City, notably John Held, Jr., Hal Burrows, Jack Sears, and William Crawford (Galbraith). The Youngs loved to entertain and became known for their large and lavish Thanksgiving dinners.

As he had in Paris, Young turned again to the theme of the common laborer. Following his first New York pieces, *The Halt and the Blind* and *Reading the Headlines*, came *Organ Grinder*. This almost pathetic little figure has an expressive realism closely associated with the painting of such artists as John Sloan and other members of the Ashcan school. Critic Charles Caffen found it "grotesque, but so

MAHONRI YOUNG SCULPTING
PETER NEWELL, CA. 1911-12
(PHOTOGRAPHIC ARCHIVES,
HAROLD B. LEE LIBRARY,
BRIGHAM YOUNG UNIVERSITY,
PROVO, UTAH)

First Snow at Leonia, 1916
etching, 8″ x 10″
(© courtesy Museum of Art,
Brigham Young University.

Organ Grinder, 1911

Piper at the Gates of Dawn, 1911

*In 1911 Young did a series of
small figures of fauns and Pan.
During this time mythological
subjects were popular.*

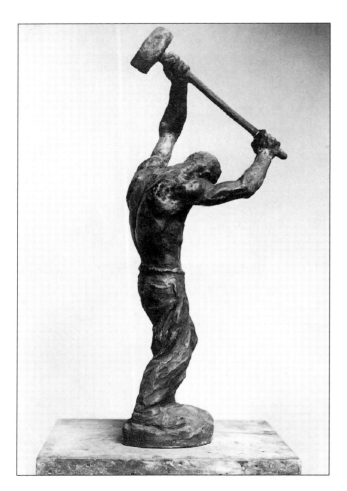

Man with a Heavy Sledge, 1911-12
BRONZE, 28 1/2″
(PHOTOGRAPHIC ARCHIVES,
HAROLD B. LEE LIBRARY,
BRIGHAM YOUNG UNIVERSITY,
PROVO, UTAH)

human and withal so expressively sculptural in the designed rudeness of its technique."[7]

Young's decision to return to labor and his career in general received a boost in March 1911 when his *Bovet-Arthur—A Laborer* won the prestigious Helen Foster Barnett prize for sculpture in the National Academy of Design's annual show. The same work also received an honorable mention in a show in Buenos Aires.

In 1912 the Metropolitan Museum of Art acquired Young's *Stevedore* and the National Academy of Design elected him an associate member. That same year an article focusing on his sculptures of laborers appeared in *The International Studio*, a prominent American art periodical.[8] Young began to be known as America's sculptor of laborers, undoubtedly influencing his decision to return to this theme. As a result, between 1911 and 1920 he produced some of his best-known sculptures.

The inspiration for one of Young's first important early works, *Man with a Heavy Sledge,* had come to him during his second year in New York City. As he contemplated his floundering career while waiting for his 5:00 p.m. drawing session to begin, he remembered an image from his days at the Art Students League, a worker with a sledge hammer whose image he had drawn from the window while looking at the street below. Encouraged by the recent success of *Bovet-Arthur—A Laborer*, he pursued this idea and hired a young Jewish refugee from Czarist Russia who had come to his studio seeking employment as a model. Young worked throughout the winter of 1911-12 on *Man with a Heavy Sledge.* When it was completed, he made a plaster mold and had it cast in bronze. The statue's bare-backed figure displays tensed muscles as the young man lifts a sledge hammer high over his head, ready to deliver a powerful blow.

In 1915 a companion piece was produced by modifying the plaster cast. Through a technique he used several times during his career, changing and altering various parts of the original sculpture, he created a new piece, *Man with a Pick.* In this work the position of the arms is changed and the head is tilted forward, giving the figure a greater feeling of forward movement. When completed, he painted the plaster cast to look like bronze.

In 1919 Rumsey Gallery on 39th Street exhibited both works, placing them on either side of the doors leading into the main studio. The sculptures sold early in the exhibit: *Man with a Pick* to a Mrs. Edward Harriman, *Man with a Heavy Sledge* to the Detroit Museum. To the artist's dismay, the plaster sculpture was knocked from its pedestal during the show. Presented with twenty-two pieces, Young pieced the sculpture together and had it cast in bronze. Mrs. Harriman later donated this piece to the Metropolitan Museum of Art where it remains a part of that museum's collection.[9]

One of Young's finest small bronzes was *Man with a Wheelbarrow.* Depicting a worker pushing his loaded barrow up what seems to be a ramp, the figure strains under the force as he moves up the incline. Although different in pose, the angle of the figure and surface modeling are reminiscent of Young's *Stevedore.*

The last major laborer Young sculpted during this period was a small statuette he called *The Rigger,* based on a drawing in his sketchbook. One day the artist had drawn a man picking up a block and tackle at a construction site outside the south window of his studio. Later he began to model a figure from the sketch, using the likeness of close friend and fellow artist Paul Dougherty when it came time to do the face. In his journal Young recorded that he had originally called this "The Iron

Man with a Pick, 1915
BRONZE, 28 1/2"
(COURTESY THE METROPOLITAN
MUSEUM OF ART. GIFT OF
MRS. EDWARD H. HARRIMAN, 1918)

Man with a Wheelbarrow, 1915

BRONZE, 15 1/4″ (COLLECTION OF
THE WHITNEY MUSEUM OF
AMERICAN ART, NEW YORK. GIFT OF
GERTRUDE VANDERBILT WHITNEY.)

Worker." With time the building being constructed next door reached the level of the artist's studio window. One day when a construction worker looked in and saw the statue, he exclaimed that the artist had done a rigger.

In another example of modification, Young later transformed *The Rigger* into an American World War I artillery soldier. Although the poses of the two figures are identical, Young took away the rigger's block and tackle and gave him a soldier's uniform.[10] The artist based this work on what he saw from life. But the pose for *The Rigger* is almost identical to George Grey Barnard's standing nude figure in *The Struggle of the Two Natures of Man.* Barnard was a sculptor Young always admired.

By now a prominent sculptor of workers, Young received a commission in 1914 dealing with industry. The next year San Francisco hosted the Panama-Pacific International Exposition that coincided with the official opening of the Panama Canal. Given his national reputation, as well as the fact that he was from the West, Young was a logical choice to do sculpture for the façade of the Palace of Manufactures and the Palace of Liberal Arts located on either side of the Tower of Jewels.

The idea for the fair was originally conceived in 1904, but the great earthquake and fire of 1906 interrupted progress. For the next several years arrangements for the exhibition moved slowly while the city was rebuilt. By the time the architect had completed his plans in 1912, the exposition had expanded to include not only a celebration of the Panama Canal which opened in 1914 but a tribute to the rebuilding of the city as well, a symbol of San Francisco's renaissance. With imaginative architecture and electric lights for the first time at an exposition, it became known as "the Jewel City." Nearly a year-long affair, it officially opened on February 20 and closed in early December 1915.

Young's commission was to create a frieze over each arch representing industries of various kinds, the spinning wheel, the anvil and forge—the work of women as well as of men. In the niche on the left he placed a woman with a spindle, on the right a workman with a sledge hammer. This presented a simple but strong visual impression.[11] Young also entered a piece in the exposition's fine arts show where he won the Silver Medal for Sculpture.

Even before his commission for the San Francisco Exposition, Young was at work on a large-scale project dealing with the theme of industry and labor. In 1911 the artist was commissioned to do reliefs and free standing figures for the façade

The Rigger, 1916
BRONZE, 26 5/8″
(PHOTOGRAPHIC ARCHIVES,
HAROLD B. LEE LIBRARY,
BRIGHAM YOUNG UNIVERSITY
PROVO, UTAH)

Metallurgy, 1912-17, CONCRETE, MONUMENTAL

Carpentery, 1912-17, CONCRETE, MONUMENTAL

Blacksmithing, 1912-17, CONCRETE, MONUMENTAL

of the new Technical High School in Salt Lake City. He had always envisioned his laborers on a monumental scale but had never been able to accomplish his goal because of prohibitive costs. Although he sculpted large figures for the Panama-Pacific International Exposition and again for the New York World's Fair of 1939, in both instances the sculptures were made of staff material, a combination of plaster and straw, and were not meant to be permanent. His only lasting, large-scale sculptures of workers are those he sculpted for the Technical High School, later the industrial arts building of West High School in Salt Lake City.

The Technical High School project which occupied the artist for several years consisted of three large reliefs depicting *Metallurgy, Carpentry,* and *Blacksmithing,* as well as four monumental sculptures: *Man Sawing, The Blacksmith, The Potter,* and *Man Pounding.* The same figures are repeated on the other side of the building, a total of six reliefs and eight statues. The three reliefs created a frieze that runs across the upper central portion of the structure. Two over-life-sized figures occupy either side of the relief portion: *Man Pounding* and *Man Sawing* on the left, *The Blacksmith* and *The Potter* on the right. The building was designed by local architects Cannon and Fetzer, and the sculptures were cast in concrete by Otto Beuhner and Co. of Salt Lake City. The fact that they are of concrete and meant to be seen from a distance explains their lack of fine detail. Two small bronzes of 1912's *Man Sawing* and *Man Pounding* are preliminary studies for this commission and show a sense of detail lacking in the

larger work. They are some of the most massively muscled figures Young ever did and exude a strong physical presence and powerful sense of force.

Through the decade Young's circle of friends and patrons increased as his reputation grew. After his show at Rumsey Gallery, the Rumseys invited the Youngs to their estate, Wheatly Hills. Artists Paul Dougherty, Arthur B. Davies, and Frederick MacMonnies, as well as philosopher John Dewey, attended the event. MacMonnies, then sixty years old, was playing tennis when the Youngs arrived. Though wet and sweaty, he spoke to the guests he knew and was introduced to others, after which he stripped naked and swam the length of the pool.[12] Young met other wealthy art patrons, including Harry Paine and Gertrude Vanderbilt Whitney, who invited him to their homes.

In 1917 Young and Gertrude Vanderbilt Whitney were both involved in doing major sculptures for the *Victory Arch* in New York City. This temporary structure was erected on Madison Square to honor returning soldiers from Europe. Young did two prominent reliefs depicting the Battle of the Marne and the Battle of Chateau Thierry. Young also did a very unusual work for its time—a statuette of an African-American infantryman carrying a rifle. *The Angry Saxon* or *The Buffalo* of 1918 was exhibited in Harlem to help promote the sale of Liberty Bonds. The next year it was included in an exhibit of American art at the Luxembourg Museum in Paris. The figure is strong and defiant. Throughout his life, Young abhorred racism and social injustice.[13]

At the time of Young's first success in New York he again introduced his proposal for the Sea Gull Monument to Mormon church leaders. The Sea Gull Monument meant everything to him, he explained to Presiding Bishop Charles W. Nibley,

Man Pounding—Stone, 1912-17

CONCRETE, MONUMENTAL
PHOTOS ABOVE AND OPPOSITE
BY CRAIG LAW

Man Sawing—Wood, 1912-17

CONCRETE, MONUMENTAL

The Potter—Clay, 1912-17

CONCRETE, MONUMENTAL

The Blacksmith—Metal, 1912-17

CONCRETE, MONUMENTAL

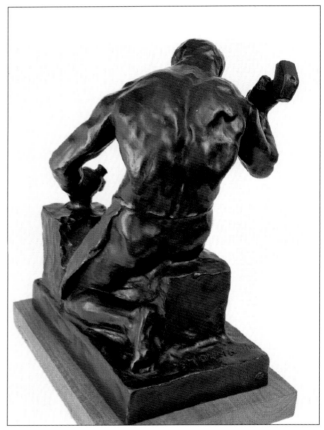

The Angry Saxon OR
The Buffalo, 1918

BRONZE, 23 1/2″
(PHOTOGRAPHIC ARCHIVES,
HAROLD B. LEE LIBRARY,
BRIGHAM YOUNG UNIVERSITY,
PROVO, UTAH)

also saying that he felt the idea would be accepted. He proposed an advance of $200 a month to live on. Church leaders accepted these terms and a contract was signed.[14] Elated, Young spent most of the summer of 1912 working on the monument. He received the commission for the Hopi Indian exhibit from the American Museum of Natural History at about the same time, requiring him to work on both projects simultaneously.

The Sea Gull Monument consists of a twenty-ton rectangular granite base from which rises a graceful fifteen-foot high doric column surmounted by a granite globe. For the top of the globe Young sculpted a pair of 500-pound bronze sea gulls with wings spanning eight feet. The birds, despite their size, appear almost weightless, as if just about to light atop the sphere. On three sides of the rectangular base, bronze reliefs entitled *The Founding of the Commonwealth*, *The Arrival of the Sea Gulls*, and *The First Harvest* tell the sea gull story. On the fourth side, a plaque is inscribed with the following words of Brigham H. Roberts: "SEA GULL MONUMENT, ERECTED IN GRATEFUL REMEMBRANCE OF THE MERCY OF GOD TO THE MORMON PIONEERS."

The three reliefs that visually tell the story of the gulls are some of the finest work Young ever accomplished. On the east side is *The Founding of the Commonwealth*. Here is depicted the arrival of the pioneers and their first efforts to cultivate and settle the land. In the left foreground a man plows the unyielding virgin soil while a young boy walks alongside driving the yoke of oxen. Directly behind them another man with his back toward the viewer seeds the newly-plowed soil. To the right a woman prepares a meal in front of their wagon home, while in the immediate foreground an Indian sits in a graceful pose. In B. H. Roberts's dated but romantic words, this symbolizes savagery giving way to civilization. In the background the majestic Wasatch Mountains loom over the valley floor.

The relief on the south, *The Arrival of the Sea Gulls*, tells the legend of the impending devastation of the crops and the arrival of the sea gulls. In the left foreground there is a figure of a man sinking to his knees, exhausted, resigned to the fact that he has failed. While he acquiesces, the woman holding a young child in hand stands with her head uplifted as if she already realizes what the arrival of the gulls means. He represents despair, she hope. In the background is a low mountain peak and a glimpse of the Great Salt Lake. All around these figures the air is filled and the ground covered with gulls as they devour the crickets. Here Young gives a silent but powerful tribute to pioneer women. In describing this scene, Roberts wrote:

> Strange that to woman—man's complement—is given such superior strength in hours of severest trial! Where man's strength and courage and fighting ends, woman's hope and faith and trust seem to spring into newness of life. From her nature she seems able to do this inconsistent yet true thing—to hope against hope, and ask till she receives. . . . [S]he, too, is toil-worn, and there is something truly pathetic in her body-weariness. But her head is raised . . .[15]

This figure of a powerful and statuesque woman with child in hand would later be used by Young for his Pioneer Woman Memorial entry. Women have a special place in Young's art. Although they appear much less frequently than men, they have the same strength and power. In the Sea Gull Monument they have their own place and work. As builders of God's kingdom on earth, they are man's equal if not superior. As twentieth-century American novelist and historian Wallace Stegner said: "I shall try to present them in their terms and judge them in mine. That I do not accept the faith that possessed

SEA GULL MONUMENT, 1912-13

BRONZE AND GRANITE, 30′
(PHOTOGRAPHIC ARCHIVES,
HAROLD B. LEE LIBRARY,
BRIGHAM YOUNG UNIVERSITY,
PROVO, UTAH)

them does not mean I doubt their frequent devotion and heroism in its service. Especially their women. Their women were incredible."[16]

The third relief, *The First Harvest*, represents the culmination of the settlers' struggle as they joyously reap their crops. To the right a seated mother nurses her baby, while at her feet a young child sits playing. This work and toil is not only for themselves but for future generations. To the left a man with a scythe harvests the grain, while in the center other men and women join in. The harvester shows all the skill and technique of any of Young's early laborers. The body moves gracefully, yet the muscles are tense and powerful. In the background

The Founding of the Commonwealth
SEA GULL MONUMENT, 1912-13

BRONZE, 50″ x 60″
TEMPLE SQUARE, SALT LAKE
CITY, UTAH (MUSEUM OF
CHURCH HISTORY AND ART,
THE CHURCH OF JESUS CHRIST
OF LATTER-DAY SAINTS,
SALT LAKE CITY, UTAH)

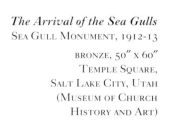

The Arrival of the Sea Gulls
SEA GULL MONUMENT, 1912-13

BRONZE, 50″ x 60″
TEMPLE SQUARE,
SALT LAKE CITY, UTAH
(MUSEUM OF CHURCH
HISTORY AND ART)

The First Harvest
SEA GULL MONUMENT, 1912-13

BRONZE, 50″ X 60″
TEMPLE SQUARE, SALT
LAKE CITY, UTAH
PHOTO BY CRAIG LAW

a log cabin replaces the covered wagon as a permanent dwelling place and home. A familiar landmark, Ensign Peak, rises in the distance.

When the Sea Gull Monument was still in progress, Young travelled to Arizona to do preliminary work for the Hopi exhibit. On the way home he stopped in Salt Lake City to make recommendations on where to place the Sea Gull Monument. This caused him a great deal of concern, for several sites had been suggested. The most popular proposed location was just south of the Salt Lake temple. Young adamantly objected. In comparison to the temple, he felt that the Sea Gull Monument would be dwarfed if placed next to it.

Church president Joseph F. Smith and other leaders met the artist. Together they walked around Temple Square viewing and discussing various sites. Young selected a spot between the tabernacle and the Assembly Hall near the south gate of the square, where the monument would readily be seen upon entering the grounds. Because he believed the sky provided the proper background for the gulls atop the monument, he wanted a clear patch of sky. Successfully persuading those with him to his point of view, he personally drove the stake marking the spot for the monument.[17]

This was one of the most important commissions of Young's early career. Representing an artistic culmination of all that preceded this work, the monument incorporated and synthesized the two sculptural themes that dominated his early career— his strong Mormon heritage and the theme of labor.

In the sculpture portion of the monument one sees the same influences as in Young's other work, particularly the Rodinesque handling and modeling of the surfaces. The figure of the man in the left-hand corner of *The Arrival of the Sea Gulls* is reminiscent of Rodin's *Thinker*. Like *Thinker*,

DEDICATION OF THE SEA GULL MONUMENT (PHOTOGRAPHIC ARCHIVES, HAROLD B. LEE LIBRARY, BRIGHAM YOUNG UNIVERSITY, PROVO, UTAH)

The unveiling ceremony took place on Wednesday, October 1, 1913.

Young's figure suggests a feeling of resignation and despair.

A more specific prototype for this figure can be found in Constantin Meunier's free-standing sculpture, *The Miner*. Throughout his life Young collected articles and pictures of this artist's work. The Meunier figure symbolizes the exhausted miner, the Young relief the exhausted pioneer. Comparing *The First Harvest* bronze relief of the Sea Gull Monument with Meunier's harvest relief on his Monument to Labor, both feature strong, stout figures that work the grain fields and share a common monumental feeling.

In the sea gull reliefs, Young proved himself a master at creating the illusion of great vistas and depth, which is a quality not found in Meunier's work. In this Young resembles the Renaissance masters, particularly Donatello, who he so admired after discovering him on his trips to Italy.

In many ways the Sea Gull Monument became the realization of his dream of a monument to labor, as well as his tribute to his own pioneer heritage, and stands as the culmination of his early career. As his son Mahonri Sharp Young said,

> The real break in his career, the foundation of all that followed, was the Seagull Monument in Temple Square, Salt Lake City. It is one of the first works; it is probably his most notable work and it made him famous. It has a lyric grace that is unique. The seagulls on the top of the column show that rare mastery of motion which he always possessed. The bas-reliefs, besides their technical virtuosity, have a touching emotional quality. Subject and artist were perfectly matched.[18]

The Sea Gull Monument enhanced Young's professional acclaim, but more importantly, as he said years later, it brought him greater satisfaction than any other commission up to that time. Well received in Utah, it helped keep his reputation

alive back in Salt Lake City and would open the door to several important commissions later. Young always considered this one of his finest works. Over two decades later he used it to illustrate the entry he wrote for the *Encyclopedia Britannica* on sculpture and sculpting. Furthermore, in 1913 Young exhibited several plaster casts of the reliefs in one of the most famous exhibitions in the history of American art—the Armory Show.

Young's association with this show was both a natural extension of his work and the result of contacts with individual artists over many years. He knew George Luks as early as 1902 in Paris. In 1903 he met Arthur B. Davies through his wife Pauline Grew, a previous close friend in Park City, Utah. In 1905 Young was introduced to Robert Henri in New York City.[19] Even before he was invited to join the association, he had become a friend of William Glackens. Of Glackens Young later reminisced:

> He like so many self centered persons had many friends and innumerable admirers. The artists closest to him were his greatest admirers. Among these were Robert Henri, George Luks, as far as it was possible for him to admire anyone except Geo G. [George Bellows], Ernest Lawson, Everet Shinn [and] John Sloan. These men were all very close to him [Glackens] from early days most of them were school mates with him at the Pennsylvania Academy.[20]

The show's official title was the International Exhibition of Modern Art. Because it was held in the Sixty-ninth Regiment Armory in New York City, it has since been referred to as the Armory Show. The exhibition's purpose was to expose the general public to the new art movements of the century. So many critics, academicians, and members of the conservative National Academy of Design opposed this new art that up to this time had little exposure in the United States. Robert Henri

Street Workers, 1910
GRAPHITE ON PAPER, 4″ X 5 3/4″
(MSS. 4, SKETCHBOOK 19,
PHOTOGRAPHIC ARCHIVES,
HAROLD B. LEE LIBRARY,
BRIGHAM YOUNG UNIVERSITY,
PROVO, UTAH)

and the Group of Eight were involved in organizing the association that sponsored the exhibit. When the group first met, they called themselves the Association of American Painters and Sculptors. Members included painters William Glackens, Ernest Lawson, Robert Henri, George Bellows, John Sloan, Maurice Prendergast, Walt Kuhn, and Arthur B. Davies. Among the sculptors were Jo Davidson, Gutzon Borglum, and Mahonri Young. Davies was elected president. He and Walt Kuhn spent the summer of 1912 in Europe where, with the aid of Alfred Maurer and the critic Walter Pach, they selected works from most of the modern art movements of Europe. Davies's plan was to show the evolution of modern art since the romantic period. The show would include works by impressionists Delacroix, Ingres, Corot, and Courbet; and post-impressionists Cézanne, van Gogh, and Gauguin. The largest section, making up two-thirds of the show, was to be works by American artists, which, when compared with modern European art, were still very conservative. These works where chosen by William Glackens.

What the exhibition is most remembered for, however, was the art of the new European modernists represented by Picasso, Braque, Matisse, Brancusi, Duchamp, Kandinsky, Picabia, and Léger. This art caused a sensation, and in particular Marcel Duchamp's *Nude Descending a Staircase* was singled out for ridicule by the press. All this negative publicity only peaked the public's interest and made it one of the most attended shows for its time in the history of American art. Over 70,000 people saw the

exhibit before a much smaller version traveled to Chicago.

Young was among the last to be admitted into the group. About its original membership in 1912, Milton Brown says, "The final make-up of the organization included also Jo Davidson, Sherry E. Fry, and Mahonri Young, all sculptors, who had probably been invited by the board of directors after the entire slate proposed by Borglum had declined election."[21] Young attended the 8 March 1913 "Beefsteak" dinner for the press, hosted by the association in conjunction with the Armory Show. Young and other members autographed the program; he appears in the press photo next to Bellows and Henri.[22]

Young was present when the association disbanded in 1914, not long after the conclusion of the Armory Show. Arthur B. Davies convened a meeting of the original organizers to announce a large deficit.

THE ARTIST WORKING IN HIS STUDIO, CA. 1918 (PHOTOGRAPHIC ARCHIVES, HAROLD B. LEE LIBRARY, BRIGHAM YOUNG UNIVERSITY, PROVO, UTAH)

Here Young poses as he sculpts a laborer with a heavy mallet. In his studio he is surrounded by his work. In the lower left-hand corner is The Chiseler *(1903), while on the shelf above are several of the artist's laborers,* The Rigger *(1916),* Man with a Pick *(1915), and* Bovet-Arthur— A Laborer *(1904). Directly behind the artist are his inspiration and muse,* Rembrandt with a Palette *(1912), which he exhibited in the Armory Show of 1913, and the beautiful portrait of his wife* Cecelia *(1906). Both appear often in photographs of his studio. To the right are plasters of a garden fountain with storks and a wall fountain of about 1917.*

In response to his request for financial support, the entire membership of the committee resigned. In *Artist in Manhattan* Jerome Myers recorded that when the final report of the Armory Show was laid on the table, "Guy duBois was the first to look at it. Shrugging his shoulders, he said simply, 'I resign.' Robert Henri followed, with the same procedure and conclusion: then likewise George Bellows, Mahonri Young and several others, including myself."[23] Young's account differs in that he resigned later, which is what actually happened. In speaking of the meeting and Glackens, he wrote:

> I saw him during the Armory Show, but the time I remember most vividly was at the final break up of the organization. There was a meeting where there was to be a final settlement and pay off. The meeting was stormy. Henri, George Bellow and their crowd resigned in a huff and walked out. Glackens did not resign. Neither did I. I don't know what Glackens motives were, but mine I knew had to do with the financial success of the exposition. There must have been an enormous surplus. No account that I ever heard of was ever made. But from that time some members seems to be well healed.[24]

Young's autobiographical notes mention little else about the Armory Show, and few of the artists ever wrote about it. Kuhn and duBois who "committed their memories to print, seemed to have wanted to forget and make no mention of the meeting."[25] The strongest impact was on the public and the press, while most of the organizers seem to have had mixed feelings about the whole affair. The Armory Show had only a minor effect on the artists and their work and almost none on the sculptors involved. "For American sculptors, the Armory Show passed with hardly a ripple of interest."[26]

Concurrent with the successful negotiations for the Sea Gull Monument contract in 1912, Young received a commission from the American

Museum of Natural History in New York City. He became involved through his old Paris roommate Howard McCormick, who now lived in Leonia, New Jersey. McCormick's next door neighbor, the assistant curator of the museum's Indian Department, asked McCormick if he would be interested in helping with a proposed Hopi Indian exhibit. McCormick, a painter, indicated he was interested in doing the landscape background but that the sculptured figures did not interest him. He suggested that Young would be an excellent choice. Young first heard about the project in the hallway of the old Salmagundi Club in New York:

> Howard McCormick called me over and introduced me to Dr. Pliny Earle Goddard of the American Museum of Natural History with these words [to Dr. Goddard], "this is the man you want to see." Dr. Goddard went on to say that the museum wanted to do some habitat groups of Indians. "Mr. McCormick tells me that you are just the man to do this. Would you be interested?" "I should say I would!" it was arranged and we were to meet at his office and talk it over.[27]

Having been in New York a year without work, Young was excited. He had always been interested in this subject and was well aware of its potential as a theme for the artist, having seen the success it brought Cyrus Dallin and others. He had personally been interested in Native Americans ever since his childhood at the factory. His first home was built with a wall for protection against possible Indian attacks. Although no real danger existed by the 1880s, Young vividly remembered that the threat of being carried off was good enough to keep the children safely inside factory compounds.[28]

In 1884, after the move to town, the family made a last visit to the Deseret Woolen Mills after they sold it. There Mahonri and his cousin Howard Snelgrove found an old pair of pruning shears with which Howard accidentally cut off the tip of the first finger of Mahonri's left hand. Hon's uncle Tom Mackintosh, one of the few members of the Young family who used tobacco, made a tobacco poultice and applied it to his nephew's finger. When it healed, Hon believed the poultice had cured his finger. Concerned about exposing the boy to vice, Hon's mother and grandmother warned him that smoking would stunt his growth. Nevertheless Hon began collecting cards that came inside cigarette packs depicting soldiers of various nations and Indians in full costume. The latter were his favorite. Fascinated by the cards, he discovered a way to expand his collection. Another uncle, Ed Mackintosh, smoked Vanity Fair, a brand that came in a pink box with collector cards of women's legs. Hon was not especially interested in the leg cards at his age, so he traded them for Indian cards. Soon he had a good-sized collection.[29]

Nationally, since the end of the nineteenth century, Americans had become increasingly interested in the Southwest and its native inhabitants. Much of the popularity came as a result of the Atcheson, Topeka, and Santa Fe Railroad, extensive advertising, and promotion of the area as a tourist destination. This was done by commissioning artists to paint Southwest scenes for railway stations and offices. These were reproduced on company calendars, brochures, menus, and train folders. The area's incredible natural beauty and the long-romanticized view of its native inhabitants gave the Southwest an exotic mystique. Anthropologists felt an urgency to collect as much information as they could about the culture before it was lost to modernity.

When Young and McCormick went to the museum, they met with doctors Goddard and Wessler, the assistant curator and the head of the Indian Department. The two artists were asked to construct

a model to serve as a proposal for the project. With the aid of McCormick's photographs, the artists prepared a model. Pleased with the results, the museum's Indian Department awarded them "small sums of money" for expenses and instructed them to begin as soon as possible.[30]

The commission took Young west and gave him first-hand experience with the Native Americans. The work expanded into representations of a total of three groups of Indian dwellings, authentically researched during three trips to the Southwest for preliminary studies.

At the beginning of the Hopi project, Young was still occupied with the Sea Gull Monument. He stayed in New York during the summer of 1912 while McCormick went to New Mexico. In the fall Young planned to meet him at La Junta, Colorado, but when he got there, there was a message at the telegraph office for him to go on to Gallup, New Mexico. At Gallup they met and from there traveled to Ganado, Arizona. Public transportation was all but nonexistent, so they made the trip in a buckboard pulled by a span of "rat size" mules, "sloshing" along for thirteen hours in pouring rain. At Ganado they met Roman Hubbel and his family who ran the now famous Hubbel trading post. This became their base camp and the artists quickly became close friends with the Hubbels who provided guides and helpful information.

Young loved the country and people. He had never seen a place that provided so many interesting things to draw. At one point in the trip they attended a snake dance, one of the most famous southwest Indian ceremonies, and saw among the guests the mayor of Chicago. He also met Bob Chanler, another artist, and related the following story:

At the dance itself, Bob was so anxious to see it all and not miss anything—he pushed himself

Navajo Woman and Herd

Hopi Snake Dance I, CA. 1924
OIL ON CANVAS, 29″ x 29″
(© COURTESY MUSEUM OF ART,
BRIGHAM YOUNG UNIVERSITY.
ALL RIGHTS RESERVED.)

through the crowd and sat down in the front row. When the dance was in full swing and the snakes were being deposited on the ground and released to crawl about until picked up by the snake-tenders, some of them came very close to the spectators before they were picked up. One especially large, fat rattler was headed right for Bob. When he was within a few feet Bob could stand it no longer and lit out a yell, Take it away! Take it away! and started to get up and get out. But, he was too slow. Before he had gotten off the ground the snake tender swept down with a large graceful movement, gathered up the snake, just back of the head, and swung it right across Bob's face. He couldn't get out of there quick enough. I next saw him on the top of a two story house, perfectly content to see it from there.[31]

The ceremony, caught by the artist in sketches, became the source for prints and paintings.

Throughout the trip McCormick took photographs while Young chose to draw. Tourists often asked why he did not carry a camera. He told them he did not need one. Those who saw his work agreed. Explaining why a sketch is better, he said, "If you look at this little sketch you will see that I have noted most of the important characteristics

Haying at Ganado, 1917-18
ETCHING, 5 3/16" x 13 1/2"
(COURTESY NORA ECCLES
HARRISON MUSEUM OF ART,
UTAH STATE UNIVERSITY)
PHOTO BY CRAIG LAW.

and actions. If I should want to use this drawing in a picture or an etching I could, while if I had only a snap shot I would have a hard time keeping the effect."[32] He made the following comment on Frederic Remington's action drawings:

> In more than one of his drawings the too close reliance on the camera is very unpleasantly apparent. Malformations are recorded due to the distortions of the lens in the foreshortening, and only too often the ends sought—movement and truth—are defeated by copying something which passes too swift for the eye to detect and where a certain static quality, due to the absolute stoppage of the action by the camera, is shown.[33]

The hundreds of drawings and sketches Young made provided the visual material for the sculptures he would do later, back at his studio at the American Museum of Natural History.

With their preliminary research completed, the artists returned to New York. As previously noted,

Young stopped in Salt Lake City to argue his choice for the location of the Sea Gull Monument. Once home in New York, he set to work to complete the Hopi group which was installed in 1914. The sculptures, of various sizes depending on whether they were in the foreground or background, were done in plaster and painted to look life-like.

The Hopi Habitat Group display was approximately twenty-seven feet long by eighteen feet high. Figures closest to the observer were approximately life-sized. In this exhibit, depicting the Hopi village of Walpi, two women and a young girl in the foreground go about their daily routine of food preparation, while to the right and in the background others go about various activities such as weaving. Corn and tobacco hang from rafters overhead to dry. Beyond the open front of the terrace, the painted background depicts the other buildings of the village bathed in a brilliant Southwest sun.

The museum immediately asked Young and McCormick to do a second exhibit, this time of Apache Indians. By the time Young could begin, McCormick had already completed the landscape background using the setting of the Santa Clara Res-

NAVAJO WOMEN

GRAPHITE ON PAPER, 4 3/4″ x 5 1/2″
(MSS. 4, SKETCHBOOK 15, PHOTOGRAPHIC
ARCHIVES, HAROLD B. LEE LIBRARY,
BRIGHAM YOUNG UNIVERSITY, PROVO, UTAH)

*Young was a great draftsman. Here
with a few lines he has caught the movement
and grace of these figures as they move
accross the deseret plain.*

HOPI SKETCH

GRAPHITE ON PAPER, 5 1/2″ x 9″
(MSS. 4, SKETCHBOOK 14, PHOTOGRAPHIC
ARCHIVES, HAROLD B. LEE LIBRARY,
BRIGHAM YOUNG UNIVERSITY, PROVO, UTAH)

*"This woman is plastering the wall
with adobe mud using her hand as a trowel."
No aspect of daily life escaped the
artist's attention.*

ervation, which Young had never seen. This created artistic problems, for Young would have to adapt his figures to the already existing background. Because McCormick had already finished his work, and Young did not want to make the trip alone, he travelled to the Southwest in 1915 with John Held, Jr.[34]

They began again at Gallup, New Mexico, travelling by mail truck, which proved to be as uncomfortable as by buckboard. The truck was so laden that Held was obliged to ride astride a saddle placed on the mail sacks, along with two young Navajos. Young who was older and heavier rode in the truck with the driver. By the time they arrived, Held was so sun-and-wind burned that the only way he could find relief was to spread a can of salad oil over his arms and face.

Roman Hubbel was not at home when they

arrived so they stayed with the Day family. All were excited to see the artist again. Hubbel arrived later and took Young and Held for a ride in his Model T. As Young later recounted: "We ended up at a whore house way out in the sage. We only entered. Roman asked if someone was there. We looked around. What a miserable lot of poor females were gathered there . . . I should think that a man would have to have been out on the desert or in the hills a very long time to satisfy his urge on any one of them."[35] Obviously Young was not interested. They stayed in Ganado long enough for Young to do some preliminary work for a possible Navajo exhibit, then went on to Polacca and the Hopi Reservation.

Being in Hopi country again was like a homecoming. Young was greeted warmly and stopped to visit and renew acquaintances from his earlier trip.

HOPI HABITAT GROUP, 1912-14
PAINTED PLASTER, 18′ X 27′
(COURTESY AMERICAN MUSEUM
OF NATURAL HISTORY,
DEPARTMENT LIBRARY SERVICES,
NEW YORK. NEG. NO. 34627)
PHOTO BY JULIUS KIRSCHNER, 1915

To his surprise, most of the locals still remembered him. The chief, in particular, treated the artist as a dignitary, which pleased him very much. They did not stay as long as they would have liked because they had to move on to Apache country.

At Holbrook, Young and Held caught a stagecoach, the only public transportation to the White River Apache Reservation. He vividly remembered his first impression: "As we approached White River, passing over a sage brush flat, where the road was straight from here, we saw approaching us three riders on horseback. We knew they were Apaches and that fact gave me a definite thrill—almost a fear."[36] They arrived safely and were welcomed by the Indian superintendent who provided them with room and board:

Then began for me a period of intense occupa-
tion, sketching, taking snapshots and observation.
It was all new to me. And, though I knew the
Hopi and the Navajos, these men and woman
were quite different. They were different in
type. They wore their hair in a different way and
they dressed differently . . . I noticed that their
hair, which the men wore long, down their backs,
had a definite brown cast. The women did theirs
up, in a sort of braid, studded with brass tacks,
but quite unlike the hairdos of the Navajos.[37]

Young worked tirelessly, surpassing his goal of
completing one hundred drawings. He returned
with over three hundred, having averaged over ten a
day, many containing several figures.[38] Startled to
find out just how different the Apache were from
the Hopi and Navajo, he carefully noted the distinc-
tions. Older Apaches still wore the traditional dress,
including the shin-length doeskin moccasin which
the artist admired. Before leaving the reservation he
traded his shoes for a pair of moccasins. He seems to
have been intrigued and charmed by the Apache
and their ways. One day while he was sitting in front
of the trading post:

> A fine looking man came in to buy something.
> His hair was very long and worn down his back.
> It was beautifully kept, brushed and combed. I
> noticed there was a slight wave in it. . . . I asked
> this man if he'd let me make a photo of him. I'd
> give him a dollar. "Sure," he said. So I took the
> shot and handed him a dollar. He stuck it in the
> pocket of his overalls and as he turned to go, in
> almost perfect English and with that wonderful
> smile of the Apache, said, "That's the easiest
> dollar I ever earned."[39]

Before returning to New York, Young and Held
went deer hunting, having been offered a hunting
guide, an interpreter, and Apache horses for the
hunt. Young had not ridden in several years and
had gained weight. Determined to prove he was a

APACHE SKETCH, CA 1914

GRAPHITE ON PAPER, 8″ x 6″
(MSS. 4, SKETCHBOOK 18, PHOTOGRAPHIC
ARCHIVES, HAROLD B. LEE LIBRARY,
BRIGHAM YOUNG UNIVERSITY, PROVO, UTAH)

*"[This] was the Apache who remarked after I
had paid him a dollar for posing for a photo,
'That's the easiest dollar I ever earned.'"*

NAVAJO HABITAT GROUP, 1916-24
DETAIL, FAMILY GROUP AND NIGHT CHANT
PAINTED PLASTER 18′ X 24′
(AMERICAN MUSEUM OF NATURAL
HISTORY, COURTESY DEPARTMENT
LIBRARY SERVICES, NEG. NO. 310796)
PHOTO BY JULIUS KIRSCHNER, 1924

westerner and not an eastern dude, he stayed with the hunt in the saddle all day, then remarked that this convinced him he made the right decision in becoming an artist rather than a rancher.

After many trips to the region, Young concluded that to preserve the land, man-made roads should be filled in, except for the main highways, and people should be required to walk or ride horseback. "The greatest menace to our parks and canyons today," he said, "is that every bit of scenery is in danger of being lost because someone, for no good reason, wishes to put an auto road somewhere."[40] As a result of his sojourn with Native Americans, he came to understand aspects of their

ways and admired their past achievements. Under favorable conditions, he said, almost anything might reasonably be expected of the Indian people in the future.[41]

As the two artists prepared to return to New York, Young's brother Wally sent word from San Francisco that Mahonri had won the silver medal for sculpture at the Panama-Pacific International Exposition. Through his work for the *San Francisco Chronicle* Wally knew the directors of the show. With this good news, Young and Held decided on a detour to see the fair because they were already relatively close to San Francisco.[42]

Young's Apache project, which was similar to the Hopi group, was well received. Sheltered from the hot sun by a grass-and-stick-covered shade, the Apache are involved in their daily duties. In the foreground a woman sits with her baby in a cradle-board. Directly behind her a man fashions an arrow. To the right another woman works on a large clay

APACHE HABITAT GROUP, 1914-16
PAINTED PLASTER, 18′ X 27′
(AMERICAN MUSEUM OF NATURAL
HISTORY, COURTESY DEPARTMENT
LIBRARY SERVICES, NEG. 36554)
PHOTO BY JULIUS KIRSCHNER, 1917

Navajos on Horseback, CA. 1916
GRAPHITE ON PAPER, 7″ X 9″
(MSS. 4, SKETCHBOOK 15, PHOTOGRAPHIC
ARCHIVES, HAROLD B. LEE LIBRARY,
BRIGHAM YOUNG UNIVERSITY, PROVO, UTAH)

NAVAJO HABITAT GROUP, 1916-24
DETAIL, MEDICINE LODGE WITH SAND
PAINTINGS USED IN CURING THE SICK

PAINTED PLASTER (DESTROYED), 18' X 24'
(AMERICAN MUSEUM OF NATURAL
HISTORY, COURTESY DEPARTMENT
OF LIBRARY SERVICES, NEG. NO. 310797)
PHOTO BY JULIUS KIRSCHNER, 1924

pot. In the immediate background a woman stands thatching a hogan, while to the left a man rides by on a horse. This scene takes place on a mesa overlooking an expansive valley below. In both the Hopi and Apache groups, a drop-off creates a natural division between foreground and painted background.

As a result of their previous successes, in the fall of 1916 Fredini Augustus Lucas, director of the museum, asked Young and McCormick to do a Navajo group and asked that they present a proposal. The artists had done studies of the Navajo on previous trips in anticipation of such a commission, so they had no trouble working up a model for which they were paid $250. In February 1917 their proposal was accepted. They immediately made plans for another trip West. Young planned to leave as soon as the Apache group was installed in the spring. However, a serious complication arose. His wife Cecelia became ill with breast cancer. Young was reluctant to leave, but Cecelia did not want him to lose the Navajo commission and urged him to return to Arizona.

After he left, Cecelia's condition worsened. We know from her letters that although her husband did not consider himself a churchgoer and made no pretense to piety, Cecelia was deeply religious. She requested that Jack Sears find a Mormon elder to assist him in blessing her. She hoped to have the pain lessened and to be allowed to live until she could see her husband again.[43] Her condition did not improve. Although she regretted interfering with Mahonri's work in Arizona, she finally sent for him. She knew she was dying.

Nearly two years earlier, the Youngs had hired an African-American maid named Betty Ann Hilton. She and Cecelia became best friends and trusted each other completely. Aware that she was leaving her children, Cecelia asked Betty to care for them when she was gone.[44]

Mahonri returned in time to see Cecelia before she passed away in 1917. As he observed her final moments, he knelt by the bedside holding her hand as the doctor and Jack and Florence Sears looked on.[45]

Young took her body to Salt Lake City for burial in the family plot. He travelled by train, numb with grief. Later he could not remember having spoken with anyone. At the funeral he requested Beethoven and Brahms funeral marches on the piano in honor of his wife's talent as a pianist. He later wrote that her loss was immense. He felt

NAVAJO SKETCH, CA. 1916
PEN AND INK ON PAPER, 7″ X 4″
(MSS. 4, SKETCHBOOK 15,
PHOTOGRAPHIC ARCHIVES,
HAROLD B. LEE LIBRARY,
BRIGHAM YOUNG UNIVERSITY,
PROVO, UTAH)

much like Tallyrand when he said, "I have little to fight for but much to endure."[46]

Betty Ann Hilton became vital to the Young household. In Young's absence during the funeral in Salt Lake City, Mrs. Net Eldridge, whose two brothers had each married one of Cecelia's older sisters, offered to have the children stay with her in Brooklyn. When Young returned a month later, he saw the severe black and white clothes that his daughter Agnes was wearing, her hair drawn back in a tight braid. He was upset to see her that way. With the children's mother gone, nothing must happen to them, he vowed. He brought the children home for Betty to care for, as Cecelia had wished, "They couldn't have been in better hands," their father wrote in his journal.[47]

Betty lived with the Youngs until failing health prevented her from going with the family to Paris in 1925. Even though she was no longer in his employ, because her health problems made a steady income impossible, Young sent money on several occasions and gave her part-time work whenever possible. Loving Betty as a family member, he believed she had organizational capabilities and a remarkable mind even though she could barely read and could write only her name. Young later wrote that because of her race and sex, society relegated her public service to religious work in her church. Young noted that African Americans were usually the last hired in the lowest paying, hardest, and most unpleasant jobs. Believing that government exists to alleviate suffering and to improve human conditions, and that the true end of government is to attempt to right wrongs, Young became critical of government inaction on racial issues. His empathy for African Americans was reflected in his later portrait of boxer Joe Gans.

Finally in 1920 Young returned to Arizona. Agnes stayed in Salt Lake City with Grandmother Young, while Mahonri and his son went on to Arizona. Mahonri loved the Southwest. Next to Paris, he loved the reservation better than any place on earth, for it reminded him of his childhood days at the factory:

> I found in that part of Arizona north of Santa Fe, conditions completely to my taste; a large landscape, vast spaces; the hills, not too high and big; small ancient trees—pinions and cedars, full of character—small enough not to dwarf man and his animals, and in this enchanting land people living primitive lives, tending sheep and goats, riding horses and burros, raising corn and wearing beautiful clothes. I have sometimes regretted not living my life there.[48]

After completing his studies, he vacationed in Salt Lake City with his family, after which the Youngs returned to New York to work on the commission. Although largely completed in 1920, the Navajo group was not unveiled until 1924 due to budget considerations.

Unlike the Hopi and Apache groups, the Navajo exhibit represents more than a scene of everyday life. This group includes a depiction of a tribal religious ceremony, an important function in the life of Navajo people. In the foreground a Navajo woman sits with her baby in her arms, preparing something over a cooking fire, a young girl looking on. Behind the woman, a seated man intently watches the tribal ceremony in the immediate background. A woman in the background to the right walks away with her dog. Ceremonial figures include a naked youth, undoubtedly the object of the ceremony, followed by the tribal medicine man and other important tribal figures. Although artistically representative of the Navajo people, a ceremony such as this would not occur simultaneously with food preparation or other household activities.

The three commissions for the American Museum of Natural History provided Young with financial security for nearly a decade. More than this, these trips to the Southwest gave him artistic inspiration for works in all media. The drawings done during this time, besides being voluminous, are some of his finest. Mahonri Sharp Young, having accompanied his father on his last trip for the museum, later wrote, "The results can be seen in hundreds upon hundreds of works. Those trips ranked among the most important experiences of his life."[49]

Young did the sculptures in New York City. At least part of the time, especially in the case of the

Navajo commission, the museum provided him a studio where he worked from the hundreds of sketches and drawings.

Admired for their realism and authenticity,[50] as one newspaper reported, in the three exhibits the sculpted figures "seem to have been taken unaware at their regular daily indoor occupations." Unfortunately the exhibits were subsequently dismantled; only photographs exist.[51] Nevertheless for some time after their installation they must have been the pride of the museum for they appeared in museum calendars throughout the 1920s.

In these exhibits Young created an accurate and

Indian Girl with Papoose, 1912-15
BRONZE, 9 3/8″
(© COURTESY MUSEUM OF ART,
BRIGHAM YOUNG UNIVERSITY.
ALL RIGHTS RESERVED.)

sensitive depiction of southwest life. "Here without effort," wrote C. Lewis Hind, "you are transported to Arizona; here you live the life of the Indians as they live today, as they have always lived—the nomadic and the sedentary—and you have the satisfaction of knowing that these are no wild-west, show-booth re-creations, but the actual facts by artists trained to observe and to translate."[52]

Realistic in the truest sense, Young's portrayal of the harsh desert life is unique for a time that otherwise romantically portrayed Native Americans as "noble savages." Numerous artists, notably Cyrus Dallin, represented this theme. Nevertheless Young's style never fell under Dallin's influence, nor under the romantic interpretation in general.

Young cast several small bronzes of individual Native American figures between 1912 and 1915. Several like *Hopi Woman* correspond to specific figures in the Hopi display. Others like *Indian Girl with a Papoose* are more general adaptations. These small statuettes show the artist's intent and what he meant to portray. The woman is accurately portrayed and authentically dressed. More than merely museum manikins, Young caught a sensitivity and psychological depth in the mother's face and demeanor. These works are not romanticized but have a sense of unvarnished realism and integrity.

Because the displays were since dismantled, they are not among his best-known works. Young's sculptures for the museum are often overlooked or have been completely forgotten. But they survive vicariously in the multitude of drawings, prints, and paintings that resulted from his preliminary studies. They attest to his versatility as an artist and skill as a draftsman. The works resulting from his excursions make this one of his most creative and productive periods.

Even after the commissions were completed,

Young made three more trips to the Southwest to sketch and paint there: one in 1929, another in 1941, and a final trip in 1950 when he was seventy-three. On one of these later trips, one of his close friends related the following:

> One day, while enthusiastically painting a desert scene Mahonri was confronted by a group of hot, hungry and weary tourists who had stopped their car not far from where he was working. One woman squinted her eyes, looked far out into the desert, raised her arms and wiped her sleeve across her perspiring face, and said disgustedly. "Well, I must say, I certainly do not see any beauty in this desert." Mahonri looked up and quietly remarked, "Lady don't you wish you could?"[53]

——

Life is short, art is long;
Only the Young can sculpt the strong. [54]

——

Notes

1. Mahonri M. Young, "Notes at the Beginning," Mahonri Young Collection, Mss. 4, box 6, folder 42, Archives and Manuscripts, Harold B. Lee Library, Brigham Young University, Provo, Utah.

2. Young, "Eighty Street and Broadway," box 5, folder 50.

3. Young, "John Held, Jr.," box 6, folder 7; Young, "Eighty Street and Broadway."

4. Young, "Dougherty, Paul and Casco Bay," box 5, folder 44.

5. Young, "Chinatown and the Hon Young Tong," box 5, folder 26.

6. Young, "Notes at the Beginning."

7. Quoted in "Mahonri Young's Artistic Search for the Rhythm of Labor," *Current Opinion* 57 (Sept. 1914): 201.

8. J. Lester Lewing, "The Bronzes of Mahonri Young," *The International Studio* 47 (1912): 76-79.

9. Young, "Heavy Sledge and Man with a Pick," box 6, folder 6.

10. See Wayne Kendall Hinton, "A Biographical History of Mahonri M. Young, A Western American Artist," Ph.D. diss., Brigham Young University, 1974, 163-64.

11. Ben Macomber, *The Jewel City* (San Francisco, 1915), 33-34.

12. Young, "MacMonnies, Frederick," box 6, folder 28.

13. See Janis Conner and Joel Rosenkranz, *Rediscoveries in American Sculpture: Studio Works, 1893-1939* (Austin: University of Texas Press, 1989), 182; Tom Armstrong et al., *200 Years of American Sculpture* (New York: Whitney Museum of American Art, 1976), 133-34.

14. Young to Charles W. Nibley, July 12, 1912, archives, Historical Department, Church of Jesus Christ of Latter-day Saints, Salt Lake City, Utah.

15. B. H. Roberts, *A Comprehensive History of The Church of Jesus Christ of Latter-day Saints* (Provo, UT: Brigham Young University Press, 1965), 3:354.

16. Wallace Stegner, *The Gathering of Zion: The Story of the Mormon Trail* (Lincoln: University of Nebraska Press, 1981), 13.

17. Young, "Miscellaneous," box 6, folder 38.

18. Mahonri Sharp Young, *Brigham Young University and M. Knoedler and Company Inc. present an exhibition of sculpture, painting, and drawing of Mahonri M. Young from the Brigham Young University Art Collection, 1969* (n.p., 1969).

19. Young, "Trip Home, 1903 and 1905," box 7, folder 18.

20. Young, "Glackens, William J.," box 5, folder 63.

21. Milton W. Brown, *The Story of the Armory Show* (New York: Joseph H. Hirshhorn Foundation, n.d.), 35.

22. Ibid., following introduction.

23. Jerome Myers, *Artist in Manhattan* (New York, 1930), 32-34.

24. Young, "Glackens, William J."

25. Brown, 199.

26. Daniel Robbins, "Statues to Sculpture from the 90s to the 30s," in Armstrong, 117.

27. Young, "Hopi Country and Ganado 1912 Trip," box 6, folder 11.

28. Young, "The Factory," box 5, folder 54; Young, "Notes at the Beginning."

29. Young, "The Factory."

30. Young, "Hopi Country and Ganado 1912 Trip."

31. Young, "Bob Chanler," box 5, folder 25.

32. Young, "Gallup, La Junta, and Ganado," box 5, folder 58.

33. Young, "Remington, Frederic," box 7, folder 4.

34. Young, "Apache Indians," box 5, folder 4.

35. Ibid.

36. Ibid.

37. Ibid.

38. Ibid.

39. Ibid.

40. Hinton, 136.

41. Ibid., 134.

42. Young, "Apache Indians."

43. Hinton, 138.

44. Young, "Hilton, Betty Ann," box 6, folder 9.

45. Young, "Sharp, Cecelia (Death of)," box 7, folder 12.

46. Young, "Notes at the Beginning."

47. Young, "Hilton, Betty Ann."

48. Young, "Notes at the Beginning."

49. Young, *Brigham Young University.*

50. Lewis C. Hind, "Mahonri Young's Drawings," *International Studio* 64 (Apr. 1918): 54.

51. No one at the museum seems to know what happened to the sculptures after they were taken down.

52. Hind, 54.

53. Jack Sears, Mss. 1058, box 3, Jack Sears Collection, Archives and Manuscripts, Lee Library.

54. This short poem is from the artist's autobiographical notes, Mss. 4, box 6, folder 37, Lee Library.

CHAPTER SEVEN.

From Paris to Hollywood

Those were golden days.

—Mahonri Sharp Young

The "Roaring Twenties" were prosperous, not only for the country but for Mahonri Young as well. He returned twice to his "favorite of all cities," Paris, which was a mecca for writers and artists from both sides of the Atlantic. Soon Young was among old friends and was again producing some of his best work.

In New York City in 1923 Young received a major commission to sculpt a Monument to the Dead in honor of fallen U.S. World War I soldiers. It was to be installed in the cloister of the American Cathedral of the Holy Trinity (American-Pro Cathedral). The architect in charge of the project was Bertram Goodhue. Known for his Gothic revival architecture, his major commissions include buildings at Princeton University, the military academy at West Point, and several major churches throughout the country. Goodhue was in transition at the time, moving toward art deco—a style he would soon use in his Nebraska State Capitol and Los Angeles central library designs.

Young met the architect at the Century Club in

Manhattan where Goodhue asked if Young would be interested in working for him, since Lee Lowrie, the sculptor he usually employed, had other commitments. Young admired Goodhue's work but knew his reputation for being difficult. Friends warned Young against accepting the commission since Goodhue, they said, would take charge and expect Young to kowtow. Nevertheless Young accepted; he would later regret this.[1]

Goodhue's proposal to Young was to sculpt an over-life-sized allegorical figure of Columbia holding a large sword. Five small figures representing artillery, infantry, cavalry, aviation, and nursing would complete the commission. There would be three scenes of French towns in bas-relief at the base which would be sculpted by another artist.

At the time Young was heavily involved with the Navajo exhibit but took time to do the preliminary studies and full-scale plasters for Goodhue in the museum studio. Goodhue approved the five smaller figures without changes. But the figure of *Columbia* signaled trouble. Though Young made suggested

Columbia, 1921-23
MONUMENT TO THE DEAD

PLASTER, MONUMENTAL
(PHOTOGRAPHIC ARCHIVES, HAROLD B. LEE LIBRARY,
BRIGHAM YOUNG UNIVERSITY, PROVO, UTAH)

*This is the full scale plaster model from which the marble statue
was carved. This photo was most likely taken in his studio at the
American Museum of Natural History in New York City.*

alterations, nothing seemed to satisfy the architect. Goodhue finally asked if Lee Lowrie could see the statue. Already frustrated by Goodhue's control over his work, Young was insulted but agreed.

Lowrie was born in Germany and raised in Chicago. During his early training he worked as an assistant in the studio of Augustus Saint-Gaudens and from there had spent a good share of his professional career working with Goodhue. During the 1920s he would become a major proponent of art deco style, employing clean, bold forms with stylized architectural flourishes. Among his most notable works are decorations for New York City's Rockefeller Center completed in the 1930s.

Goodhue, Lowrie, and Young met to discuss the project but were unable to come to any conclusions. Finally Lowrie suggested that he and Young meet alone. In Goodhue's absence, Lowrie and Young changed the helmet, dress, and hair, which Goodhue had specifically instructed Young not to change. By the time the commission was finished, Young felt that the piece was significantly compromised. Later he called Goodhue a "little czar" and vowed he would never work with him again.[2]

After completing the full-scale plaster model to Goodhue's satisfaction, Young had it shipped to Paris and then followed as soon as he had finished his Navajo group. He stayed four months, supervising the cutting and sculpting of the final figure in stone. Most of this work was done by assistants and stone-cutters, giving him time to reacquaint himself with the city. Calling the stint in Paris his "vacation of vacations," Young was surprised to find so many of his American friends all in one place. He mentions visiting with Lee Richards, Paul Dougherty, Jack Sears, Guy Pène duBois, Ernest Lawson, Herman Webster, Paul Manship, Hester Bancroft, Mary Tarleton, and Harry and Grant Reynolds.[3] He

stayed until the dedication of the monument,
which for him was an exciting experience complete
with the highest diplomatic corp officials from
France, England, and the United States.[4]

When he returned to New York City for the
installation of the Navajo group, he still had not
received the last payment of $1,000 for the Monument to the Dead. Goodhue had once told him, "I
[have] never finished any work for a church but
what I have [had] to . . . threaten to sue for the last
payment." Finally Young mentioned to the monument committee that he had found an attorney to
assist him. Young received his money the next day.[5]

Despite Lowrie's changes in minor details of
dress and head gear, the figure of *Columbia* is basically as Young envisioned her. The statue serves as
part of the architectural setting, rising out of a protruding corner of which she is an integral part. This
is a continuation of the Gothic tradition of combining sculpture and architecture, in this case in the
art deco style. The ornate Gothic ornamentation
around the figure's head complements the setting
and helps create a natural niche for her. Stylistically her regal elegance reminds one of a Gothic
jamb statue, while the simplified and angular treatment of the drapery and modeling can be compared to contemporary art deco statuary.

For a number of reasons the Monument to the
Dead is unique among Young's work. Due to the
extensive collaboration and intervention involved
in the project, it is atypical of his style. This was
one of his few commissions executed in stone, and
the only work that was planned specifically as part
of an interior architectural setting.

It is apparent that this was a collaboration, as
the figure of *Columbia* is done in Art Deco while
the Gothic tracery that frames the top of her head
and the rest of the monument are much more

MONUMENT TO THE DEAD, 1921-23
MARBLE, MONUMENTAL
AMERICAN CATHEDRAL OF THE
HOLY TRINITY (AMERICAN PRO
CATHEDRAL), PARIS (PHOTOGRAPHIC
ARCHIVES, HAROLD B. LEE LIBRARY,
BRIGHAM YOUNG UNIVERSITY,
PROVO, UTAH)

Rolling His Own, 1923
BRONZE, 13 1/4″
(© COURTESY MUSEUM OF ART,
BRIGHAM YOUNG UNIVERSITY.
ALL RIGHTS RESERVED.)

bronze depicts a stereotypical cowboy. With his jaunty pose, he is all decked out in appropriate attire—chaps, six-gun, bandanna, and hat—as he rolls himself a cigarette. The most notable variation of this figure depicted the same cowboy holding a branding iron. *Rolling His Own* and *The Branding Iron* capture an underlying emphasis on the harmony and beauty of the human figure, with their classical contrapposto and natural feeling of relaxation. In this respect they are reminiscent of *Bovet-Arthur—A Laborer*.

During this time Young became involved with another project dealing with the American west. In 1926 Ernest W. Marland, governor of Oklahoma, oil man, and philanthropist, conceived a grand monument to "the pioneer woman." Marland invited twelve of the most prominent American sculptors to submit a bronze statuette to be considered for the memorial. Those who participated were James Earle Fraser, Hermon Atkin MacNeil, A. Sterling Calder, Jo Davidson, John Gregory, F. Lynn Jenkins, Bryant Baker, Wheeler Williams, Maurice Sterne, Mario J. Korbel, Arthur Lee, and Mahonri Young. Each was awarded $2,000 to cover expenses. In this unusual competition, the final decision was made by popular vote. Before the seventeen-foot-high monument would be erected in Ponca City, Oklahoma, the twelve models were sent on a tour of twelve major cities: New York, Boston, Philadelphia, Pittsburgh, Detroit, Chicago, Minneapolis, St. Paul, Dallas, Fort Worth, Oklahoma City, and Ponca City. The winner of the contest would be decided democratically, though it is interesting, for a Western statue, how few of the cities were Western. The winner would then be commissioned to reproduce his entry monumentally.[6]

The people's choice by almost a two-to-one margin was Bryant Baker's work. F. Lynn Jenkins's

traditional. After completing the Monument to the Dead in Paris, no large commissions came Young's way for a time, so he maintained himself and his family by teaching at the Art Students League.

After his return from Paris in 1923, Young turned his talents to a western theme, the American cowboy. The result was his first small bronzes of a western subject in almost a decade. The most successful Young called *Rolling His Own*. This

The Pavers, CA. 1923
OIL ON CANVAS, 30″ x 48″
(© COURTESY MUSEUM OF ART,
BRIGHAM YOUNG UNIVERSITY.
ALL RIGHTS RESERVED.)

bronze was the second most favorite, and John Gregory's the third. When he learned that he had not won, Young was discouraged because the theme of the pioneer woman was close to his heart. Later he said that this was the greatest disappointment of his career.[7] Still the experience gave him publicity and broad exposure.[8]

Baker had used a professional actress as his model, which produced a glamorous figure, representing Western myth more than reality. In contrast, Young's *Pioneer Woman* is strong and monumental— a figure of substance combined with classical restraint in the tradition of Millet. Young sculpts a pioneer woman capable of the rigors and hardships of frontier life, though also sensitive and feminine. He focused on the universal theme of mother and child, creating a Madonna of the Plains. A precedent for the statue exists in the Sea Gull Monument. As in the earlier work, the woman is full-

figured and stately and holds an infant in her left arm, while a child stands close to her on the right holding her hand. The figure has a presence and stately elegance reminiscent of a Piero della Francesca. She holds her child in the embrace of a Renaissance Madonna.

Young made a model showing his concept for the entire monument, including a large base with a raised platform. This provided a walk-around area from which the statue could have been viewed from all sides. At the front was to be a monumental staircase flanked by two enormous bison, while around the base would be scenes in relief depicting episodes from the settling of the West. If Young's

BOTH ABOVE:
PIONEER WOMAN MEMORIAL, 1926, PLASTER
(PHOTOGRAPHIC ARCHIVES, HAROLD B. LEE LIBRARY,
BRIGHAM YOUNG UNIVERSITY, PROVO, UTAH)

Pioneer Woman Memorial had been erected, the overall effect would have been one of classical monumentality. Despite his disappointment, several concepts and features from this work would later appear in his This is the Place Monument.

Young was entering one of the most productive periods of his career. In 1925 Eldridge Adams offered to become a patron if Young would repay him in art, and Young readily accepted. Since it did not matter to Adams where he lived or worked, he decided to move the family to Paris. In that artistic environment—in the companionship of dear friends such as Leo Stein, Paul Dougherty, and Paul Manship—and with the economic freedom Adams's support allowed, Young would later say that "those were golden days."[9] While in Paris Young celebrated his fiftieth birthday. About this milestone he wrote: "[A]t fifty, with nothing assured, and only a little done, I am surprised at my calmness."[10] He sculpted some of his best sculptures and produced a flood of drawings and sketches. The artist's son later wrote: "[I]n 1925 he moved over with his children for a stay of two and one-half years. This was among the most fruitful periods of his life; he was freed from teaching and from the pressures of commissions, and he had again the great advantage of working in an atmosphere where art was important and natural."[11]

Young made the move late in the summer of 1925 and rented Paul Manship's Paris studio at 17 rue Campagne-Premiere. Young not only spent time in the city but made excursions into the country. At the coastal town of Dieppe he sketched the people he saw going about their daily activities. Women peddling their wares inspired two bronzes: *Porteuse du Poisson* (Fish Seller) and *Porteuse du Pain* (Bread Seller). In general, the poses, hair, and dress are similar in both figures. The subtle variations in pose

Pioneer Woman, 1926
BRONZE, 36″
(PHOTOGRAPHIC ARCHIVES,
HAROLD B. LEE LIBRARY,
BRIGHAM YOUNG UNIVERSITY,
PROVO, UTAH)

were intentional so that when the two figures are placed side by side they seem to be deep in conversation as they walk along. Young called this piece *The Gossips*. This and other works were cast separately and with small modifications also as a group.

Young's favorite spot was the Ide d'Ouessant which he visited with Dana Pond and Paul Dougherty. Impressed with the rugged coastline and the violent storms, the artists took long walks,

Ouessant Shepherdess, CA. 1925-26

OIL ON CANVAS, 20″ X 29″
(© COURTESY MUSEUM OF ART,
BRIGHAM YOUNG UNIVERSITY.
ALL RIGHTS RESERVED.)

OPPOSITE: **The Gossips**, 1925-26

KNOWN AS *Porteuse du Poisson* (LEFT) AND
Porteuse du Pain (RIGHT), BEFORE BEING CAST
AS A PAIR ON ONE BASE. BRONZE, 15 3/4″
(© COURTESY MUSEUM OF ART, BRIGHAM
YOUNG UNIVERSITY. ALL RIGHTS RESERVED.)

These two sculptures, Porteuse du
Poisson *(Fish Seller) and* Porteuse du
Pain *(Bread Seller) were called* The Gossips
*after being subtly modified and cast as a
pair on one base (1925-26).*

Woodcutter with Tree Stump, 1926
BRONZE, 13 5/8″
(© COURTESY MUSEUM OF ART,
BRIGHAM YOUNG UNIVERSITY.
ALL RIGHTS RESERVED.)

Woodcutter with Hooked Axe, 1926
BRONZE, 13 1/4″
(© COURTESY MUSEUM OF ART,
BRIGHAM YOUNG UNIVERSITY.
ALL RIGHTS RESERVED.)

often sketching and painting all day. Young more than once mentioned the storms and the magnificent waves.[12] Out of this experience, he produced several fine paintings, among them *Ouessant Shepherdess*. This windswept figure is reminiscent of his own Native American work and the series of paintings Winslow Homer did of women and the sea.

Inspired by the country and villages, Young did his last series of small bronzes of laborers while in France. The figures are of woodcutters. It depicts a man bent over chopping, and in this series Young varied the tool used and the object being chopped. *Woodcutter with Tree Stump* and *Woodcutter with Hooked Axe* show the similarities and differences

in this series. These figures, sinewy and tough, bend over their work with tool in hand in the act of chopping. They are common peasant types and recall the paintings of Courbet and Millet.

After he had been in Paris for almost a year, Young began his Prizefighter series. The first and best known piece, *Right to the Jaw*, was an immediate success and sold well, especially with Americans.[13] *On the Button* followed and is similar in concept and execution. Young also took a figure from *Right to the Jaw* and cast it separately as *Groggy*. These were all done in the last half of 1926 and early in 1927. After this Young was able to use reigning European middle-weight champion Rene

Devos as the model for his next major work, *The Knockdown* (1927). With this piece Young's prize-fighters become larger in scale. *The Knockdown* also shows a move away from the emphasis on dynamic movement of form and figure in space to the narrative drama of the ring—the winner and the loser. The last major sculpture Young did in Paris was *Da Winnah.* This large work combined three separate pieces, *The Winner, The Loser,* and *The Referee.* It is an interesting work and by far the most purely narrative of all the works in the series. From the front the winner stands triumphant, his taut, muscled body in stark contrast to the slick smooth surface of the ring announcer's jacket. When seen from the back, it becomes a completely different work. Here the viewer focuses on the limp, crumpled body of the defeated fighter.

Sports had been important during Young's formative Utah years. According to the artist, he and his younger brother, Wally, used to attend fights together, and it was Wally who first gave him the idea of sculpting prizefighters. Wally went on to beome a professional sports reporter in San Francisco. Many famous early fights were held in Nevada, the first state to legalize boxing. Tex Rickard, one of the most famous figures in the history of fight promotion, was associated with Utah,[14] and heavyweight Jack Dempsey hailed from the state and used to train in the old Salt Lake High School and National Guard Armory.[15] Later Young and Dempsey knew each other and Jack always refered to Mahonri as Brother Young. During his student years in Paris, Mahonri and Leo Stein liked to attend amateur boxing matches, as attested to by the drawings in his sketchbooks. In 1903, after one of these matches, Stein and Young decided to put on the gloves and go a few rounds. Young landed a hard right to Leo's forehead and felt his thumb give way. It was broken.

Groggy, 1926
BRONZE, 14 1/2"
(COURTESY COLLECTION OF WHITNEY
MUSEUM OF AMERICAN ART, NEW YORK)

Even after the splint was removed, it was difficult to sculpt. As a consequence, while his thumb healed, he turned to watercolor.[16]

Young's first exhibited work dealing with the theme of boxing was apparently in 1918 at a major show of his work at The Sculptor's Gallery in New York. The catalog included fifty-five pieces of sculpture, among them one called *Prizefighters.*[17] But it was not until 1926 in Paris that he again pursued this theme.

These prizefighter sculptures were a significant contribution to the history of American art and brought Young considerable fame as reflected in the opening sentence of a 1941 *Life* magazine

LEFT AND BELOW:
Right to the Jaw, 1926-27

BRONZE, 14″
(COURTESY NORA ECCLES
HARRISON MUSEUM OF ART,
UTAH STATE UNIVERSITY,
LOGAN, UTAH)
PHOTO BY CRAIG LAW.

OPPOSITE ABOVE:
The Knockdown, 1927

BRONZE, 23″
(© COURTESY MUSEUM OF ART,
BRIGHAM YOUNG UNIVERSITY.
ALL RIGHTS RESERVED.)

OPPOSITE BELOW:
On the Button, 1926-27

BRONZE, 13 7/8″
(© COURTESY MUSEUM OF ART,
BRIGHAM YOUNG U NIVERSITY.
ALL RIGHTS RESERVED.)

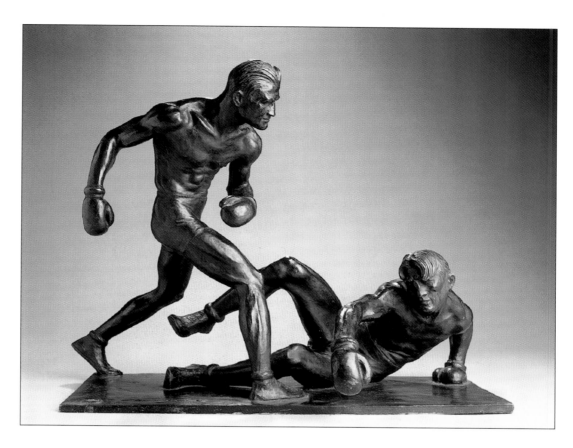

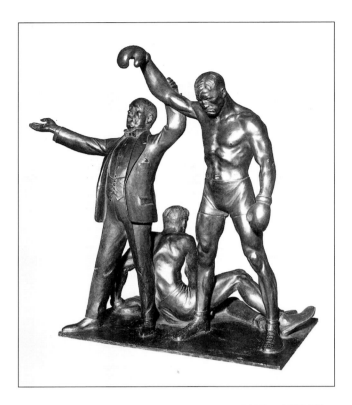

ABOVE and BELOW:
Da Winnah, 1928
BRONZE, 38"
(PHOTOGRAPHIC ARCHIVES,
HAROLD B. LEE LIBRARY,
BRIGHAM YOUNG UNIVERSITY,
PROVO, UTAH)

ning feats of individual achievement. More than in any previous era, entertainers, actors, musicians, aviators, writers, and athletes were in the limelight. Names like Charles Lindbergh, F. Scott Fitzgerald, and Babe Ruth became synonymous with the age. "In a decade dedicated largely to escapism, and general levity, sports gained the publicity which made it one of America's foremost social institutions," wrote one historian. Sporting events and sports heroes provided much of the excitement and glamour of the times. Legends like Babe Ruth, Lou Gehrig, Red Grange, Bobby Jones, Helen Wills, Jack Dempsey, and even a horse, Man of War, earned for the 1920s the title the "Golden Age of Sports."[19]

No sport gained more attention than boxing. It was evolving from an underground activity considered brutal and barbaric to a contest of style. By 1900 the center of the boxing world shifted from England to the United States, but even before this time it was popular. America's first national sports celebrity was John L. Sullivan, a bare-knuckle champion who fought before the turn of the century and made over $100,000 in the ring and over

article him: "The George Bellows of realistic American sculpture is Mahonri Young."[18] A decade earlier George Bellows, an Ashcan painter, gained prominence with his canvases of boxing matches. Young's bronze sculptures of prizefighters prompted this association. By turning to the theme during the 1920s, he ensured himself a living for several years. Through his prizefighters Young was able to create a market for his work, which he had been unable to accomplish the previous decade with his laborers. In part, the reason for this success was the country's infatuation with boxing.

The Roaring Twenties became the epitome of eternal optimism, progress, good times, and stun-

$1 million from theatrical tour lectures and a vaudeville show that paid anyone to beat him in four rounds.

In Sullivan's day there were no holds barred. Contestants decided on the number of rounds to be fought, and, if there was no knockdown, the referee decided the victor. Regulations were first introduced with the so-called Queensbury Rules for the Sullivan-Corbett title fight in 1892. Eight years later the number of rounds was standardized. With rules, the sport became more humane and was legalized in New York and Nevada for private clubs in 1897 and in New York for public viewing under the control of a state commission. Politicians began to see pugilism as a source of revenue for state and city governments. The famous Dempsey-Tunney fight was the first sporting event in history to make over $1 million at the gate.[20] Prize fighting was at the height of its popularity when Young returned to New York City in 1928 for his first major exhibition at the Rehn Gallery. The *New York Times* called his prizefighters "particularly amenable to sculptural treatment" and praised the artist's ability to give the feeling of "balance, proportion and integrated mass."[21]

Back in New York Young soon received a commission of a much different type from the Phoenix Hosiery Company. He was to sculpt a female figure in high relief, with emphasis on the legs. He used one of the Ziegfeld's Follies dancers for a model, aware that this was little more than an advertising ploy but happy for the notoriety. He told the press that he was delighted to use one of Florenz Ziegfeld's girls as a model.[22]

THE ARTIST WITH PHOENIX HOSIERY COMPANY COMMISSION, "THE LADY OF THE LEGS," 1929

PLASTER TO BE CAST IN BRONZE (PHOTOGRAPHIC ARCHIVES, HAROLD B. LEE LIBRARY, BRIGHAM YOUNG UNIVERSITY, PROVO, UTAH.)

"In 1929 the artist wrote 'Laborers, indians, cowboys, prize fighters, and now beautiful legs for a stocking ad . . . where will it all end' " (Mss. 4, box 2, folder 5). She was nicknamed "The Lady of the Legs" and appeared in the company's advertisements.

With all the seeming glitz surrounding Young, in the summer of 1929 he attracted the attention of Winfield R. Sheehan, president of 20th Century Fox Studio in Hollywood. Sheehan telephoned Young to come to California. While waiting in Sheehan's reception area, Young asked the secretary what he should ask for if hired. She said to ask for $750 a week and settle for $500. This proved to be good advice. The interview went well and Young signed a contract for $500 a week plus travel expenses for himself and his daughter Agnes. He returned to New York to get things in order for the trip, and several days before arriving in Hollywood viewed a film of the Joe Gans versus Bat Nelson fight, giving him the inspiration for a statue that would prove to be his most significant in Hollywood.

Agnes spent a week in Salt Lake City with her grandmother, then joined her father in Hollywood.[23] Wined and dined and shown the town the week of his arrival, Young wrote in his journal, "What a week, What a place."[24]

In his work for Fox, Young did sets of large, portrait-relief medallions for the Fox Studio Laboratory of Technical Research and the new Fox Studio Music Building. These included eight profile busts of famous musicians such as Mozart, Verdi, and Liszt which were placed on the music building's façade above each doorway in the recess of the arch of a false arcade. He also did art for the stage set of Paul Muni's film, *A Friend of Napoleon* and busts for *Seven Faces*,[25] another film by Muni. When not working on projects for 20th Century Fox, Young completed commissioned works for Sheehan's home and a posthumous, life-sized sculpture of African-American prizefighter Joe Gans, who held the lightweight title throughout most of the first decade of the century. This was the bronze inspired earlier by the film the artist viewed in New York of Gans in ac-

tion. During Young's brief, four-and-a-half-month stay in Hollywood, he completed seventeen pieces.

At the time the artist chose to sculpt the athlete, black fighters were an anomaly. The first to gain wide public acceptance was Joe Louis in the 1930s. Although Louis dominated the boxing world from 1935 to 1949, his manager set down the following rules: he was never to have his picture taken alongside a white woman, he was never to go into a night club alone, he was to keep a "dead pan" in front of the cameras, and he was to live a clean life.

Louis was preceded by a few black pioneers who did well in the ring despite disadvantages. Born on 25 November 1874 in Philadelphia, Gans was the first African American to win the lightweight title. During his brilliant career he was known to predict the round in which he would knock out his opponent. He was one of those rare individuals who was considered one of the greatest in his class ever to have lived.

During the athlete's career it was not uncommon to fight someone outside one's own weight class, so on occasion Gans fought heavyweights. He fought three men in succession on 15 July 1901, with one win and two draws. At the time a win implied a knockout; there was not yet such a thing as a decision win.

On 23 March 1900 Gans fought Frank Erne for the lightweight title. In the twelfth round Gans stopped, went to his corner, and requested that the fight be stopped. On 12 May 1902, in a rematch, he knocked out Erne in the first round. He retained the championship title until 1908. In his most famous fight, 3 September 1906, against Bat Nelson at Goldfield, Nevada, Gans won on a foul after thirty-two rounds. Of the $32,000 purse, he received $11,000, having agreed to give Nelson anything over that amount, win, lose, or draw.

Left to the Side, CA. 1928
OIL ON CANVAS, 20″ X 24″

Although he had never seen Gans fight, Young admired what he had accomplished. With no restrictions as to what his next work would be, he began a life-size sculpture, though he encountered difficulty finding a strong enough support for the large clay model. Two Fox Studio carpenters constructed a lead base and armature, but under the weight of the clay the lead support gave way, causing the entire figure to slip. Finally a stronger iron support frame was built.[26]

In order to sculpt a convincing likeness, Young wanted to find good photographs and a fighter who would pose for him who was about the same size and physique as Gans. Young's greatest frustration was finding action photographs. He located four

poor pictures in the Fox Studio library and some better shots from spectators, but otherwise found nothing. But as people came to see Young's work in progress, among them fans who had seen him fight, Young was able to gather helpful suggestions. One former fighter gave personal insights into Gans's personality, fighting style, and habits in the ring. The secretary of the Los Angeles Boxing Club gave suggestions regarding his movement and expressions. Young's brother Wally had interviewed Gans

THE ARTIST, HOLLYWOOD, 1929
(PHOTOGRAPHIC ARCHIVES,
HAROLD B. LEE LIBRARY,
BRIGHAM YOUNG UNIVERSITY,
PROVO, UTAH)

*The peccador and cock were done for the
Beverly Hills home of Winfield R. Sheehan,
president of 20th Century Fox Studio; the
composers Mozart, Verdi, Liszt, Grieg, Debussy,
Beethoven, Sullivan, and Tchaikovsky for 20th
Century Fox Studio Music Building; and
Alexander Graham Bell and Thomas Edison
for 20th Century Fox Studio Laboratory
of Technical Research.*

20TH CENTURY FOX
STUDIO MUSIC BUILDING
(PHOTOGRAPHIC ARCHIVES,
HAROLD B. LEE LIBRARY)

once and was able to provide additional valuable assistance. Working with these eyewitness impressions, Young completed the statue and had it cast in bronze. It was an immediate success.

The *Joe Gans* statue was displayed first in Sheehan's home, after which it went to Madison Square Garden in New York City, the nation's home of boxing from the 1920s to the 1940s, to adorn the main entrance. The statue was later moved to the Hall of Fame Club at the Garden.[27]

Young's personal friend and fellow artist George Bellows had an influence on Young's sculpture. Similarities can be seen in comparing Young's group of small bronzes entitled *Right to the Jaw,*

sculpted in 1926, with Bellows's most famous painting, *Stag at Sharkey's.* Both Young and Bellows emphasize stark realism, and each in his own medium expresses the force of the action in a dynamic manner. Bellows is more graphic and narrative and includes not only the boxers but the fans as well, with the boxers' blood and the crowd's frenzy. Young's focus is more on the athlete's aesthetic beauty when caught in motion.

The prizefighters are among the best examples of Young's technical and artistic mastery of the human form. The *Right to the Jaw* group seems to come alive, seething with action. Young once said, "To me the problem has always been to animate the inert

THE ARTIST SCULPTING *Joe Gans* IN HOLLYWOOD, 1929
(PHOTOGRAPHIC ARCHIVES, HAROLD B. LEE LIBRARY,
BRIGHAM YOUNG UNIVERSITY, PROVO, UTAH)

and lifeless material, whether bronze, stone, or wood, and to make it function like one of nature's own creations."[28] Whether it is the powerful drive and thrust of a solid right or the stunning effect of such a punch, Young convincingly models the figures in a seemingly effortless manner. The surface is still reminiscent of Rodin's influence, but, unlike Young's earlier works, the surface shows a multiplicity of subtle planes suggesting the slipping of taut muscles under the skin. This is especially apparent in the sculpture *Groggy*, which Young adapted from one of the figures in *Right to the Jaw*. The musculature appears tense, yet at the same time the boxer seems to float as if on the verge of collapse. "The

real technical analogy," critic Frank Jewett Mather, Jr., pointed out, "is not with Rodin or Meunier bronzes, but with a fine early Renaissance bronze, say an Antonio Pollaiuolo."[29]

Not only may influences be seen from Renaissance sculpture but also from classical Greece. Young particularly admired Myron's *The Discus Thrower* for a quality he referred to as the openness yet compactness of the work.

How does it achieve this quality in such a high degree? By nothing else than by line. By line it achieves its superb unity and also its marvelous sense of Movement—movement rhythmical and swift. It, in all its parts, suggests previous positions

and others to follow. Nothing is static, and yet, such is the masterly use of the interplay of lines that the statue as a statue maintains a perfect equilibrium and functions perfectly within its total space.[30]

Young's comment about Myron alludes to an important aspect of what he himself attempted. *Right to the Jaw* and *On the Button* demonstrate his ability to capture anatomical movement. Fashioned in lithe, twisted shapes, the figures are composed in sweeping curves and long opposing diagonal lines. Young's *The Knockdown*, and especially *Da Winnah*, which was inspired by ringside sketches, emphasizes the narrative drama of the fight. The postures and expressions of the defeated figures, as with the winners, tell the story that is unfolding in the ring.

Prior to going to Hollywood, Young had accepted a teaching position at Dartmouth College

for the second semester of the 1928-29 school year. He did not complete the semester for personal reasons. Since 1925 he had carried on an extensive correspondence with Mary Tarleton. During that time she wrote to say that she was in a hospital in Oklahoma, and he quit his teaching position to be with her.[31]

During his extended stay in Paris, Mahonri began spending time with Dorothy Weir. They visited the Louvre often and talked about art. She was an artist herself and the daughter of J. Alden Weir, the famous American impressionist painter who passed away in 1919. Fourteen years had passed since the death of Young's first wife, and he had gradually begun entertaining the idea of a relationship with another woman. When his close friend Mary Tarleton recovered from her illness, he returned to New York to pursue his relationship with Weir.

Young first met Dorothy Weir in the 1920s at a dinner party for artists and patrons hosted by Duncan Philips, the wealthy American collector. After Young introduced himself, he and Dorothy spent much of the evening in conversation. The next day he told his children that he had met a woman he would consider marrying. He wrote in his journal that this was probably beyond the realm of possibility, given the fact that he was an artist with two children and she a woman of wealth living on Park Avenue.[32]

The two artists met occasionally, then Dorothy invited him to dinner at her home. He arrived at her luxurious apartment too early and felt awkward the entire evening. Embarrassed, he made no attempt to see her again.

In 1927, while he was in Paris, Mahonri again met up with Dorothy. She was vacationing there with her mother, and Mrs. Weir invited Mahonri to dinner on the Right Bank. This seems to have rekindled the couple's interest in one another, since during the remainder of their time in Paris they were together often, for instance at the Louvre where they engaged in long discussions about their common interests. The relationship did not develop beyond social encounters at the time, and Young turned his attention to Tarleton in New York.

Young and Weir saw each other occasionally in New York before he went to Hollywood to work for the Fox studio in 1929. After thirteen weeks in California, Young returned to New York and began seeing Dorothy again. From this time on, their relationship became increasingly serious. One night he put his arm around her while riding in a New York cab. Then he kissed her. She protested. She told him she thought they should not see each other. He disagreed. They became engaged on 25 January and married on 17 February 1931.[33]

The Youngs spent their honeymoon in Paris, calling it a working vacation. At this time Young completed one of his best known and finest prints, *Pont Neuf*. The idea for this etching had been in the artist's mind for some time. This famous Parisian bridge had long been a favorite subject for many artists, but what made Young's work unique was its unusual point of view.

While in Paris in 1923 to complete his Monument to the Dead, Young had made a quick sketch of the bridge and put it in his pocket. Several days later he looked at it again and at least three friends commented on the unusual point of view. In the meantime he researched other artists' depictions of the bridge in order to satisfy himself that his perspective was truly unique. When he was again in Paris in 1925, he decided to do a print but never got around to it because of other projects. Finally in 1932 the work came to completion. Young did over fourteen preliminary drawings and studies. When he started etching, the first plate did not turn out so he started another which was a success.[34] This etching was selected for a "Fine Print of the Year Award" in 1934 and in 1939 was purchased for the Joseph Pennell collection of the Library of Congress.[35]

In 1932 Young sent *Joe Gans* and *The Knockdown* to the Olympic Games Exhibition in Los Angeles where *The Knockdown* won the gold medal for sculpture. The artist's name appeared on the sports page of several newspapers across the country, which he said was as satisfying as seeing it in the arts section. As a result of this exposure, he was subsequently elected president of the Society of American Sporting Art. He designed the Muldon-Tunney Heavyweight Championship Trophy which carried a $1,200 stipend.[36]

After their honeymoon, the couple moved to Branchville, Connecticut, where they lived on the old Weir farm that Dorothy inherited when her father died. Now in his fifties and Dorothy in her forties, the Youngs loved the country, where they were surrounded by fields, wooded areas, a pond large enough for boating, and farm animals. They stayed in Branchville from early spring until late fall each year, spending winters in New York City.[37] They both continued to work actively as artists.

Looking forward to the next decade the Youngs felt happy and secure. Mahonri was at the height of his career and was recognized as one of America's finest living sculptors. They had the means and the maturity to enjoy life's little pleasures while simultaneously pursuing their highest aspirations.

Notes

1. Mahonri M. Young, "Goodhue, Bertram and Lee Lowrie," Mahonri Young Collection, Mss. 4, box 6, folder 39, Archives and Manuscripts, Harold B. Lee Library, Brigham Young University, Provo, Utah.

2. Ibid.

3. Young, "Notes at the Beginning," box 6 folder 42.

4. Young, "Monument to the Dead," box 6, folder 39.

5. Young, "Monument to the Dead," "Goodhue, Bertram and Lee Lowrie," and "Paris 1901-05 and 1923-5," box 6, folder 45.

6. Patricia Broder, "The Pioneer Woman, Image in Bronze," *American Art Review* 2 (1975): 127-34.

7. Young, "Notes at the Beginning."

8. See *Deseret News*, 2 May 1936.

9. Mahonri Sharp Young, *Brigham Young University and M. Knoedler and Company Inc. present an exhibition of sculpture, painting, and drawing of Mahonri M. Young from the Brigham Young University Art Collection, 1969* (n.p., 1969).

10. Young, Journal, box 3.

11. Mahonri Sharp Young.

12. Young, "Isle de Ouessant," box 6, folder 14.

13. Young to Mary L. Tarleton, Nov. 1926, box 2, folder 2.

14. John Farnsworth Lund, "A Visit to the Champ's House," *Utah Historical Quarterly* 55 (Fall 1987): 355.

15. Virginia Rishel, ed., "The Rise of Tex Rickard as a Fight Promoter," *Utah Historical Quarterly* 55 (Fall 1987): 64.

16. Young, "Notes at the Beginning."

17. *Sculpture, Drawing, and Etchings by Mahonri Young* (New York: The Sculptor's Gallery, 1918).

18. "Mahonri Young's Sculpture Preserves His Mormon Past," *Life Magazine*, 17 Feb. 1941, 76-78.

19. *America's Sporting Heritage, 1850-1950* (N.p., n.p).

20. Douglas A. Noverr and Lawrence E. Ziewacz, *Sports in American History, 1865-1980* (Chicago: Nelson-Hall, 1983), 87-88; *Sports in the Western World* (Totowa, NJ: Rowman and Littlefield, 1982), 220-25.

21. *New York Times*, 19 Feb. 1928.

22. Young, "Notes at the Beginning."

23. Young, "Hollywood, 1929," box 6, folder 10.

24. Young, Journal, box 3.

25. *The Salt Lake Tribune*, 29 Sept. 1929; Young, "Notes at the Beginning."

26. Young, "Gans, Joe," box 5, folder 10.

27. Ibid.

28. John A. Swenson, "The Art Philosophy of Mahonri M. Young," M.A. thesis, Brigham Young University, 1971, 104.

29. Frank Jewett Mather, Jr., "The Art of Mahonri Young," *Mahonri M. Young: Retrospective Exhibition* (Andover, MA: Addison Gallery of American Art, 1940), 9.

30. Swenson, 104, from a letter to a Miss Mannes, 10 Apr. 1928.

31. Mahonri Young to Bill Young, 3 Mar. 1929, box 3, folder 3.

32. Young, "Weir, Dorothy," box 7, folder 24.

33. Ibid.

34. Young, "Etching," box 5, folder 51.

35. Young to Jack Sears, 23 Aug. 1939, Sears Collection, Mss. 1058, box 3, Archives and Manuscripts, Lee Library.

36. Young to Jack Sears, 23 Aug. 1938; Young, "Muldon-Tunney Heavyweight Championship Commission," box 7, folder 35.

37. Young to Jack Sears, 8 Aug. 1932, box 3, Sears Collection; Young, "Notes at the Beginning."

CHAPTER EIGHT.

Depression Years: Branchville, Connecticut

In consequence of all this I'm never bored;
I only lose interest when I'm tired, otherwise Art is a continual delight, trouble and irritation.

—Mahonri Young

Young was at the height of his career when in October 1929 the stock market crashed and the Great Depression began. The arts were among the first to feel the effects of the economic and political crisis, and Young was affected dramatically. Even though critics hailed his work, sales dropped and the patronage he had come to rely on all but disappeared. Letters and journals from this period record his reaction. He became critical of the general public and their ability to appreciate and value art. He could not understand why culture was considered a luxury rather than an essential part of American life. Commenting in a 1930 *New York Times* interview, he said that Americans of past generations were more educated and had a keener appreciation of beauty. He blamed the public education system.[1]

Young's marriage to Dorothy Weir brought him enough financial security that he did not have to worry about subsistence maintenance, but, as much out of pride as the need to be purposefully employed, he took a position in 1934 as Instructor of Sculpture at the Art Students League. He was not new to the league, having taught there off and on for almost two decades, but this was his first full-time position.

Throughout the rest of his career Young would continue to teach. Considered one of the best and most popular teachers on the faculty, he had some of the largest classes. He did not believe in giving grades; he had seen too many dogmatists among art school faculties. The teacher's role, in Young's mind, was to guide and inspire students, not toward a prescribed formula which he felt spelled corruption in art but rather toward students' own individual styles. He knew from experience what it took to make a living as an artist. "Art in all its branches," he once said, "is a hard career and I should never recommend it to anyone who can refrain from doing it."[2]

Early in the decade a personal tragedy struck Young that influenced him greatly. The untimely

Harness Race, Danbury Fair, 1933

death of his friend Alfred Maurer gave him cause for personal reflection. The two had remained close since their early years in Paris. Maurer began as a realist, and when he made the switch to modernism Young said that this change came to him as a conversion. After that "he was never again the gay, light-hearted Alfy his friends had known."[3] During the last part of 1931 Young saw Maurer several times in New York. The last time he saw him, Maurer was coming out of the Weyhe Gallery while Young was going in. Upon seeing his friend, Young said, "Alfy you look fine," to which Maurer replied, "Hon, I'm a very sick man." Those were the last words Young would hear from his friend, for eight months later, in 1932, he took his own life.[4] Maurer's death stunned Young; he wrote in his journal that those who commit suicide are not insane but see life at its clearest.[5]

Because of the Great Depression, this was a

turbulent time. Many artists were politi-
cally active and saw their art as a vehicle for
social protest and political reform. Young
never saw his art this way, even though his
laborers could be interpreted as having
political overtones. He did, however, have
strong political views. As a staunch sup-
porter of Franklin D. Roosevelt and his
policies, Young said, "His career gave me
back some of my lost faith in democracy
and the American people."[6] Concerned not
only with his own country, the artist was
keenly aware of developments in Europe.
From the beginning he did not trust
Adolph Hitler and said that he must be
stopped or there could be all-out war.
When Paris fell to the Nazis in June 1940,
he was deeply saddened and said that the
fall of his beloved city was the result of a
few rich French families that cared more for
their wealth and property than for France.

In 1930 Young again turned to Western subjects and produced several small bronzes. The
three most significant were all figures on horseback. *The Frontiersman* is a rustic, bearded figure
fringed in buckskin and carrying a rifle. The positioning and sculpting of the horse's legs create a
feeling of rhythmic grace and forward movement,
while the rider's arms, his left forward and right
back, mirror in opposite the horse's front legs and
create a rhythmic echo of the same motion. The
horse's head is lowered as he plods along, while the
frontiersman gestures with a pointed finger to the
trail ahead. The companion piece is a figure the
artist titled *The Pioneer*. The vested figure with
brimmed hat rides a spirited horse whose head is
up as if fighting the bit. (Later this figure would
appear on the north and south sides of the central

Riding the Girder, CA. 1932
OIL ON CANVAS, 39″ X 24″
(© COURTESY MUSEUM OF ART,
BRIGHAM YOUNG UNIVERSITY.
ALL RIGHTS RESERVED.)

*Two of New York City's major
landmarks were constructed in
the depths of the Depression: the
Empire State Building and
Rockefeller Center. In this
painting, Young has caught
the spirit of the times.*

There Lies the Trail, 1930-31
BRONZE, 16 1/2"
(PHOTOGRAPHIC ARCHIVES, HAROLD B. LEE LIBRARY,
BRIGHAM YOUNG UNIVERSITY, PROVO, UTAH)

pylon of the This is the Place Monument.) The artist combined these two sculptures to create a work called *There Lies the Trail*. In this bronze the figures play off each other beautifully. One horse's head is down with reins loose, while the other's head is up with reins tight. The frontiersman leans forward as he points out the trail ahead, while the pioneer leans back as he controls his horse. These movements and gestures combine to give this sculpture a narrative quality that unites the two figures. Young's Western sculpture represents an important and personal part of the artist's oeuvre. He never attempted to become part of a popular genre or to copy the work of other Western sculptors. His work remained personally and uniquely the product of his own vision.

Young's *Pony Express Rider* is one of his most stylized Western sculptures. Rider and horse seem joined in one fluid movement. At full gallop, with all four legs fully extended, the front brim of the rider's hat blown back, horse and rider combine to create a vision of breakneck speed. The effect is reminiscent of popular nineteenth-century English prints of horsemen on the hunt. More specifically the piece resembles the simplified style of Young's friend during this time, Paul Manship. Much like the latter's *Young Hunter and Dog* (1926), Young emphasizes the beauty of line and shape rather than realistic motion. In this aspect, Young differs from more traditional and popular artists of the West such as Frederic Remington. Comparing their work, one sees the difference in technique.

FATHER KINO MEMORIAL, 1934-35
BRONZE, 43 1/2" x 58", TUSCON, ARIZONA
(PHOTOGRAPHIC ARCHIVES, HAROLD B. LEE LIBRARY,
BRIGHAM YOUNG UNIVERSITY, PROVO, UTAH)

Remington faithfully recreates split-second action with photographic exactness, while Young places emphasis on capturing the harmony and balance between horse and rider and the feeling of fluid movement and grace of a full gallop.

Young must have liked this piece, for he incorporated it into two other small commissions—the H. R. Driggs Medallion and the 1936 International Philatelic Exhibition Plaque. In both works the figure of the rider is sculpted in relief. Interestingly the philatelic rider faces right while the medallion rider faces left.

One of the few commissions Young receive during this decade was to sculpt the monument commemorating the life of Padre Eusebio Francisco Kino. A Jesuit priest who worked as a missionary with the Pima Indians, Father Kino was one of the earliest explorers and settlers of the American Southwest. This was a satisfying assignment for Young. Since his commissions for the American Museum of Natural History, he had longed to do more Southwest themes. His interest in the Spanish fathers and explorers dates back to his earliest trips to the area. On his first trip to Ganado and the Hopi country in 1912, a Catholic priest, also an artist, gave Young a Franciscan habit. At the time, Young was working on a sculpture of Padre Junipero Serra and needed the cauled robe for his model. It later proved useful in catching the flow of Father Kino's robes.

After completing the monument in 1935, the artist travelled from New York to Tucson, Arizona,

Pony Express Rider, 1931

to attend the dedication of the memorial. The Father Kino Memorial consists of a large tablet divided into two sections, a large main upper section and a small predella-like section below.[8] The upper part, sculpted in relief, depicts Kino striding out across the desert in the midst of native flora and fauna holding the Bible in one hand and a cross in the other. The Father is led by an Indian youth carrying a bow and arrow. Around the youth's neck hangs a cross symbolic of his conversion to Christianity. Father Kino is especially strong; the artist catches the power and action of the figure and a classical stylized sense of grace in the flowing robes.

In each corner of the lower section are small scenes in relief. The center tablet contains an inscription: "PADRE-EUSEBIO-FRANCISCO-KINO. S.J. Earliest pioneer of civilization in the southwest, Heroic missionary to the Pima Indians, Intrepid explorer founder of San Xavier Del Bac."

Sculptures of animals were a favorite theme that extended throughout Young's entire career. He did many small bronzes and often incorporated animals as main features, as well as small decorative elements of many of his commissions. In the last half of the nineteenth century, sculptors, mainly Europeans called *animaliers,* used fauna to

Industry, 1938
BRONZE, 48″
(MUSEUM OF CHURCH HISTORY AND ART,
THE CHURCH OF JESUS CHRIST OF LATTER-DAY
SAINTS, SALT LAKE CITY, UTAH)

Agriculture, 1938
BRONZE, 48″
(MUSEUM OF CHURCH HISTORY AND ART)

communicate human themes and emotions. Rather than capitalize on the popularity and sentimentality of the subject, Young concentrated on creating a sense of form and special relationships. During his early career in New York, he sculpted a pair of elephant bookends that were a commercial success. Between 1914 and 1948 Gorham Company Founders alone cast 108 pairs.[9] One of his finest works from this period was *Tethered Elephant*. This small bronze depicted a wild animal in captivity, leg chained to a large stake, as the elephant pulls vigorously against his shackle. Here the artist captured a strong feeling of force and tension, reminiscent of

his laborers. The rich and roughly-modeled surface is consistent with his other works of this decade.

Duck and Shoat, a work from the 1920s, showed a dramatic change in style, one seen to a lesser extent in other sculptures from this time on in the artist's career. The surface is more smoothly modeled, the roughly-textured surface giving way to a greater emphasis on form as well as relationship of positive and negative space. This same quality can be seen in the 1930s statuette *Lunch on the Desert, Burro with Foal*. As the foal suckles, the mother turns her head; the simplicity and unity of the two figures blending to one creates not only a physical but psychological bond.

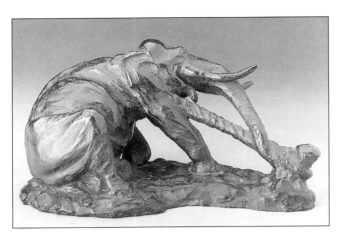

Tethered Elephant, 1914
BRONZE, 5″

Duck and Shoat, 1926
BRONZE, 6 5/16″

In 1939 Young had the opportunity to return to the theme of labor, this time on a grand scale. The majority of his laborers were small, but for the 1939 World's Fair on Long Island he was commissioned to do two fourteen-foot-tall sculptures representing *Agriculture* and *Industry*. The giant plaster-and-straw figures were placed at the entrance to the fair. *Agriculture* depicts a man sharpening a scythe, while *Industry* shows a bare-chested worker with a wrench in one hand and a large hammer slung over his shoulder. True to his own vision at a time when art deco and futuristic styles were popular, Young stayed with his rugged realism, a tribute to those who work with their hands. Not considered his best, these two pieces seem caught between the simple surface handling of the art deco style and the more rugged active surfaces of Young's earlier work.

In a century dominated by technology, automation, and science, Young insisted on placing human beings above machines, always representing the dignity of common laborers. Nevertheless, in a very traditional approach to sculpture for the year 1939—especially *Agriculture,* looking like an enlargement of a nineteenth-century mantlepiece figure— these statues lack the dynamic qualities of energy and form as well as the subtle surface modeling of the artist's smaller works.

The culminating event of Young's career in the East came in 1940. That year the Addison Gallery of American Art in Andover, Massachusetts, held a major retrospective show of Mahonri's work. The introduction to the exhibition catalog was written by eminent art critic Frank Jewett Mather, Jr., who wrote:

> I am amazed at the variety of subject matter and methods. The fine craftsmanship seems universal. Beside the alert and paradoxically elegant bronze statuettes of workers and prize fighters,

and the etchings of Western and Indian subjects, . . . here are scores of drawings, selected from thousands,— drawings in many media and on the most diverse themes, but again unified by a common powerful elegance. And there are paintings in oil and watercolor, subjects ranging from the Paris quays to the Sierras, from the prize ring to the harvest field, and all singularly immediate in conception and fresh in expression.[10]

For more than a decade Young had been involved in the struggle to save one of pioneer Utah's oldest and most venerated landmarks, the historic Salt Lake Theatre. Built in 1861-62 under the direction of Brigham Young, the theater stood as a symbol of civilization and the arts in the untamed West. When constructed, it was the first major theater between the Mississippi River and California. In 1928 the Mormon church decided to sell the theater and adjacent lots to the Mountain States Telephone and Telegraph Company for an office building. A great public outcry followed the announcement, and the sale and demolition of the theater came about amid agitated opposition. Attempts were made by civic organizations to preserve the theater. The mayor of Salt Lake City proposed that the city assume theater maintenance and upkeep. Because these efforts were rejected by church president Heber J. Grant, just before demolition, in anger and frustration, someone changed the lettering on the marquis to read, "Erected by a prophet and destroyed by a profiteer."

Young was especially upset. Even though he lived in the East and abroad, he maintained close ties with the West through friends and associates in Utah and served as a volunteer artistic advisor to Utah and the Mormon church. It saddened him that the second generation of Mormon leaders would allow the work of the first generation to be destroyed. In an undated letter to George D.

Lunch on the Desert, Burro with Foal, 1930
BRONZE, 5 3/4″
(PHOTOGRAPHIC ARCHIVES, HAROLD B. LEE LIBRARY
BRIGHAM YOUNG UNIVERSITY, PROVO, UTAH)

Agriculture, 1939
STAFF MATERIAL (DESTROYED), MONUMENTAL SIZE
LONG ISLAND ENTRANCE TO 1939 NEW YORK WORLD'S FAIR
(PHOTOGRAPHIC ARCHIVES, LEE LIBRARY)

Rowen, CA. 1938
OIL ON CANVAS, 25″ X 30″

SALT LAKE THEATRE MEMORIAL PLAQUE, 1939
BRONZE, 88″ X 50″
PHOTO BY CRAIG LAW

Oxen Pulling, Danbury Fair, 1933
OIL ON CANVAS, 60″ X 85″
(PHOTOGRAPHIC ARCHIVES,
HAROLD B. LEE LIBRARY,
BRIGHAM YOUNG UNIVERSITY,
PROVO, UTAH)

Pyper, who published a history of the theater the year it was demolished entitled *The Romance of an Old Playhouse*, Young wrote that his mother told President Grant that destroying the theater was the worst thing he ever did and that he would live to regret it. Whether he regretted it or not, it was a mistake. Two decades later the Daughters of Utah Pioneers erected a replica of the original Greek Revival-style theater, and today there are two other building façades in Salt Lake City patterned after the original.

In 1929, the year after the theater was torn down, Ada Dryer Russell, an actress who had performed there, asked Young to design a plaque commemorating the building. The artist gladly accepted the assignment. Ten years later $3,000 had been raised for the commemorative tablet. Even though Young was occupied with other work and would not make money on the commission, he executed the tablet because he felt so deeply about the destruction of the theater.[11]

The plaque is straight-forward in presentation and conservative in execution. In the center appears a relief of the old theater amid the hustle and bustle of people entering before a performance. The lower part contains an inscription. On the upper portion five classical figures represent drama, dance, and music. The gestures of the figures and stylized flow of their draperies are reminiscent of Paul Manship. The tablet was placed on the side of the telephone building near the corner of First South and State streets.

For personal reasons Young experienced a great sense of satisfaction with this work, feeling that in his own small way he had helped right an injustice. Amid an intense effort to secure Utah's This is the Place Monument commission, completion of this memorial brought him welcomed local press which praised his work. Articles continued to appear in the newspaper, bringing attention to his name and enhancing his reputation as he worked with the committee on the upcoming project—the one which would be the greatest accomplishment and greatest trial of his career.

Notes

1. *New York Times*, 13 Dec. 1930.

2. Mahonri M. Young, "Notes at the Beginning," Mahonri Young Collection Mss. 4, box 6, folder 42, Archives and Manuscripts, Harold B. Lee Library, Brigham Young University, Provo, Utah.

3. Mahonri Sharp Young, *Early American Moderns* (New York), 20.

4. Elizabeth McCausland, *A. H. Maurer* (New York: Published for the Walker Art Center, A. A. Wyn, Inc., 1951), 237.

5. Young, Journal, box 3.

6. Young, "Troubetsky, Prince Paul," box 7, folder 19.

7. Young to Dorothy Young, 6 Mar. 1933, box 3.

8. Young, "Kino, Father," box 6, folder 20.

9. Janis Conner and Joel Rosenkranz, *Rediscoveries in American Sculpture: Studio Works, 1893-1939* (Austin: University of Texas Press, 1989), 186.

10. Frank Jewett Mather, Jr., "The Art of Mahonri Young," in *Mahonri Young: Retrospective Exhibition* (Andover, MA: Addison Gallery of American Art, 1940), 7.

11. Young, "Salt Lake Theatre," box 7, folder 9.

CHAPTER NINE

This is the Place Monument: The Big Job

I have dreamed and hoped that someday Utah
could find the will and means to let me make a monument to the pioneers, adequate to
their great achievements. I would be willing to spend years of my life on it and
make it my crowning masterpiece.

—Mahonri Young

In the American West, pioneers play an important role in every state's history, but in few places are they more honored and venerated than in Utah. They are not only historically significant but a religious symbol as well. In his history of the Mormon Trail, Wallace Stegner wrote:

> For every early Saint, crossing the plains to Zion in the valleys of the mountains was not merely a journey but a rite of passage, the final, devoted, enduring act that brought one into the Kingdom. Until the railroad made the journey too easy, and until new generations born in the valley began to outnumber the immigrant Saints, their shared experience of the trail was a bond that reinforced the bonds of the faith; and it has continued to have sanctity as legend and myth.[1]

The arrival of the first Mormons in Utah marked a new beginning. The significance of the event was immediately recognized, and this collective "rite of passage" began to be commemorated in celebration. Brigham Young chose a vast unsettled basin because he felt it was a place no one else wanted, and there his followers would be protected and safe from the travails they had suffered in Missouri and Illinois. Here Zion would be built. The date of July 24, the day Brigham Young and the last of the first pioneer company finally entered the valley, became within a short time Utah's greatest annual holiday.

The first year after the pioneers' arrival the situation was too bleak for festivities. Everyone was too concerned with eking out an existence. Furthermore, their leader was not with them. Brigham had gone back to Winter Quarters in the late summer to prepare other companies to come West and did not make it back to the valley until September 1848.

The following year their situation seemed more secure, and on July 24, 1849, festivities were held that lasted the whole day, complete with a parade, picnics, and orations. The *Deseret News* recorded the events of the day as follows:

the inhabitants were awoke by the firing of cannon, accompanied by music; the brass band played and was carried through the city in two carriages. At eight o'clock the multitude were called together by the firing of guns and music. This was at the house of Brigham Young where the parade or procession was organized. The procession was lead by a brass band, and followed by twelve bishops bearing banners of their wards. Twenty-four young men [followed] dressed in white, with white scarfs on their right shoulders, and coronets on their heads, each carrying in his hands the Declaration of Independence and Constitution of the United States, and swords sheathed in their left hands; one of them carrying a beautiful banner, inscribed on it "The Zion of the Lord."

Twenty-four young ladies [came next], dressed in white, with white scarfs on their right shoulders, and a wreath of white roses on their heads, each carrying the Bible and Book of Mormon: and one bearing a very neat banner, Hail to our chieftain.

Then came the leadership and hierarchy of the Church including Brigham Young, Heber C. Kimball, and John Taylor.

Then twelve more bishops carrying banners of their wards, which were followed by twenty-four silver grays . . . each having a staff, painted red on the upper part, and a branch of white ribbon fastened at the top, one of them carrying the flag with the stars and stripes, and the inscription—Liberty and Truth.[2]

From that time on, Pioneer Day became an annual event. July naturally lent itself as a time of festivities. Crops had been planted and harvest time had not yet arrived.

With each passing year the holiday grew more elaborate and spread to every Mormon colony. In 1880, thirty-three years after settling the valley and fifty after the founding of the church, an especially large Pioneer Day was held. The parade was over three miles long and included:

The surviving Pioneers of 1847 in five wagons. Portraits of Brigham Young on both sides of the first wagon with the inscriptions "Gone Before Us" and "Absent But Not Forgotten." Above them was the "old pioneer banner," on which were the names of all the pioneers and a picture of Joseph Smith blowing a trumpet. Also the U.S. flag. Surviving members of Zion's Camp. Surviving members of the Mormon Battalion and a wagon with "Women of the Mormon Battalion." The "Minute Men." Wagon with representatives of the various countries of the earth. On the side were various mottoes.

24 couples. "The ladies looked lovely in cream-colored riding habits, with white silk caps and white feathers, and the young men presented a fine appearance in black dress suits, white neckties, and white gloves." Education was represented by a car containing five ladies personifying Religion, History, Geography, Science, and Art.[3]

In a speech at that celebration church president Wilford Woodruff recounted for the first time Brigham Young's famous "this is the place" statement which has become associated with the festivities ever since. Although Woodruff accompanied Young, neither his nor any of the other journals kept by members of the original company, nor their numerous later recountings of that famous entry into the valley, record those words. The statement nevertheless became one of those summations of a whole chapter in the history of a people. As Stegner concluded: "If in actuality it was never said it should have been."[4]

That same year Congress passed the Edmunds-Tucker Act which outlawed polygamy. This created a new challenge and caused the Latter-day Saint church to go through some of its hardest times. With this new law the government's discipline was

THE ARTIST WITH THE FINISHED *Spanish Explorers:*
Fathers Escalante and Dominguez Group, CA 1946-47

(PHOTOGRAPHIC ARCHIVES, HAROLD B. LEE LIBRARY,
BRIGHAM YOUNG UNIVERSITY, PROVO, UTAH)

swift and effective. Church property could be confiscated and church leaders still practicing polygamy were driven into hiding. This situation continued until the church issued a manifesto in 1890 ostensibly ending the practice of polygamy. The way was paved for Utah to become a state in 1896.

After statehood was obtained, Utahns, and the Mormon church in particular, strove for acceptance and to come into step with the rest of the country. In this endeavor, art played an important role. Utah pursued a course that the rest of the country had followed since the end of the Civil War in honoring their war heroes, living and fallen. The United States, especially the North, entered an unprecedented period of monument building. The war stirred a patriotic chord, and people's losses were so great that a reminder of the purpose of these sacrifices was a comfort. "After the war such sentiments were institutionalized in the north into civic monuments. Every hamlet, every village green had its war memorial or local hero in permanent stone, bronze, or cast iron, all of which kept a hoard of sculptors lucratively busy."[5]

In Utah the arts began to flourish at a new, though conservative, level as the state fell into step with the national trend. Utah had not participated in the Civil War, nor had its leaders sympathized with the North, so there was little to memorialize on a war theme. But organizations such as the Sons of and the Daughters of Utah Pioneers were formed to preserve the memory and keep the traditions of the original settlers alive, accomplished largely by placing markers and monuments at historical sites. This activity flourished at the turn of the century. Instead of parade wagons, pioneers were now put on pedestals.

The most prominent sculptors to come out of pioneer Utah were Cyrus Dallin, Gutzon and Solon Borglum, Avard Fairbanks, and Mahonri Young. Dallin's Brigham Young Monument, the first major commissioned sculpture in Utah, was produced at a time when Utah was working toward statehood. Even before it was completed, Dallin's figure was taken to Chicago in 1893 and displayed prominently in front of the Utah building at the Chicago World's Fair—Columbian Exposition. It was finally unveiled in Utah on the fiftieth anniversary of Brigham Young's entry into the valley. Fifty years later Mahonri Young's This is the Place Monument would commemorate the centennial of that event.

It is not known when the idea for a major monument to the pioneers first came into being, but the possibility of doing such a monument had been in Young's mind since early in his career. He mentioned the idea in a letter to Jack Sears, adding: "All my life I have been interested in the western migration of our people. It always seems to me to be one of the greatest epics of the world."[6]

As early as 1920 Young heard of the possibility of a 100th anniversary commemoration of the Mormons' arrival. In a letter to the artist dated July 21, 1920, Heber J. Grant, president of the LDS church, expressed regrets that Young had not been chosen to do the monument to the Mormon Battalion. A family friend for years, Grant knew Mahonri's mother and had taken an interest in his career. He acknowledged the artist's skill and ability that was so visibly evident in the Sea Gull Monument. He wrote that "as to the monument 'The Coming of the Pioneers' to be erected at the mouth of Emigration Canyon, I am afraid it is a long while in the future before this monument will be erected." He ended by reassuring Young: "Ever praying for your welfare and assurances of regard and esteem and assuring you that you can count on me for doing everything in my power to help secure you any work in your line."[7] Grant's support later proved critical in securing Young the commission.

In 1921 the Mutual Improvement Association, the church's youth group, placed a small plaque commemorating the entry of the pioneers into the valley. Then in 1930 the Utah Pioneer Trails and Landmarks Association was established specifically to propose and erect a "Coming of the Pioneers Monument." A committee began arranging for finances. George Albert Smith, a high-ranking LDS apostle, was chosen to head the committee.[8]

They chose a site at the mouth of Emigration Canyon east of downtown Salt Lake City, located on the Fort Douglas Military Reservation which came under the purview of U.S. Secretary of War George H. Dern, a former governor of Utah. To secure the property, Utah's congressional delegates drafted a bill allowing Dern to cede the land to the State of Utah. Congress passed the bill in May 1936.[9]

As these events transpired in Washington, D.C., planning continued in Utah. On July 16, 1934, an article in the *Deseret News* announced that the Utah Pioneer Trails and Landmarks Association planned to erect an "imposing monument" at a state park. The projected cost was $100,000. The article mentioned several ideas under consideration, including a proposal by Avard Fairbanks to construct a monument with a stairway and observation platform to view the valley. It was also suggested that a large museum with pioneer artifacts be built of stones from every country and state from which the early settlers of Utah had emigrated. The association promised that more definite plans for the site and monument would be forthcoming.[10]

By November 1935 the trails association had appointed another committee to work with civic and church organizations and to consider artists' proposals. At this time the Sons of Utah Pioneers suggested combining the dedication of the monument with a world's fair as part of the centennial festivities in 1947.

Young visited Salt Lake City in 1936. An old friend, prominent church and civic leader Nephi Morris, told him about the committee's effort to locate an artist. Young showed Morris his own ideas and sketches. Young had not been so excited since the onset of the Sea Gull Monument project and for "the next days, weeks, and months he thought of little else."[11]

Not only did Young gain Morris's support, but a short time later President Grant told Young, "everybody wants you to get it."[12] Young discussed his ideas with his old friends and fellow artists Lee Richards, Al Wright, and Jack Sears. He began researching historical data and made extensive sketches and studies, discussing his proposal with members of the committee. What originally started out as a short vacation ended up a five-month stay.

After doing all he could, he returned to New York, disappointed that he had not yet been able to obtain the commission, feeling only "frustration and futility."[13] Because of past experiences with committees and commissions, he knew he would have to lobby aggressively. In retrospect it was probably not the best thing to do. He imagined that he might be able to get federal backing for the monument, which would further enhance his chances of getting the job. He travelled to Washington, D.C., to speak with U.S. senators from Utah, Elbert D. Thomas and William H. King, as well as with Edward Bruce of the Treasury Art Projects, in hopes of obtaining funds.[14] By doing so he offended committee member John D. Giles.

Giles told Young that the contract could not be

awarded yet because the church did not have the financing in place. Young learned that Giles used this pretense to gain time to persuade other artists to enter into the competition. Giles approached Waldo Midgley who was a life-long friend of Young's, heightening the tension between the committee member and the artist.

In 1937 the first substantial amount of money was appropriated for the monument when the State of Utah agreed to release $125,000 over several years on condition that the church and private donors raise matching funds. By the time the monument was finished and the books closed in 1952, the total raised from other sources was $292,500 of a total cost of $453,000.[15] To Young's chagrin, the committee decided on a competition. Young tried to convince President Grant that this would not be a good way to make a selection. He had seen the results of the Pioneer Woman competition and wanted the committee to choose an artist in whom they had confidence—namely himself. He asked his cousin, Levi Edgar Young, to help persuade the committee to his point of view, but they decided on a competition. Young did all he could and concluded that "if it's to be a fight it's going to be a good one."[16] Young worked on his proposal, lobbied committee members, and tried to influence the makeup of the committee. When his friend, mayor of Salt Lake City Clarence Neslen, visited Young at his home, Young encouraged him to get himself appointed to the committee. One of the committee members was Judge William H. Reeder. In 1906 the judge's wife had attended one of Young's art classes and Young still had a drawing of her he had done. He felt that this would be a good time to send it to the judge.[17] He wrote letters to Giles, Morris, George Albert Smith, Levi Edgar Young, President Grant, and Governor Henry H. Blood

soliciting their support. He assumed that Grant would remain chair of the committee but was not alarmed when Apostle David O. McKay was selected permanent chair, for he felt he had McKay's support as well.[18]

As the battle to win the commission progressed, the competition narrowed to two men, Young and Fairbanks, both nationally-known artists representing the most famous of Utah's active sculptors. Not surprisingly Fairbanks lobbied as vigorously as Young. He had already completed two major commissions dealing with Mormon history— *The Tragedy of Winter Quarters* Memorial and The Monument to the Three Witnesses to the Book of Mormon on Temple Square.

The younger artist hailed from Provo, Utah, where he was born to John B. Fairbanks and Lilly Huish in 1897 and given the name Avard Tennyson. His father, one of Utah's prominent painters, was an instructor of art at Brigham Young Academy. Born tenth in a family of considerable artistic talent, by the time Avard was twelve, and under supervision of his older brother Leo who had studied art in Paris, the child savant sculpted a rabbit in clay that was entered in the 1909 Utah State Fair. The next year his father took him to New York City where the older Fairbanks copied famous paintings for Utah clients and Avard began copying sculptures. It was unprecedented for such a young artist to be allowed to do this. Working at the museums, Avard caught the attention of the press. *The New York Herald* published an article entitled, "Young Michelangelo . . . in Knickerbockers Working at the Metropolitan Museum." The article went on to say: "He was the youngest sculptor who has ever plied the plastic art within the walls of the Metropolitan Museum." Young Fairbanks has unusual good sense of proportion for one of his years and his work has a certain freedom indicating the true artistic instinct."[19] This acclaim, combined with the boy's skill, won him a scholarship at the Art Students League where he studied sculpture with James Earle Fraser. That year he exhibited at the National Academy of Design, the youngest artist ever to do so.

At age sixteen Avard went to Paris to continue his studies at the Ecole Nationale des Beaux Arts, the Académie de la Grande Chaumiere, the Académie Colarossi, and the Ecole Moderne. His work was exhibited at the Grand Salon. Unfortunately his time was cut short by World War I. Returning to Salt Lake City he was able to finish his formal education and continue to sculpt, exhibiting seven works in the rotunda of the Fine Arts Palace of the Panama-Pacific International Exposition in San Francisco. In 1917 he went to Hawaii to work with brother Leo on the ornamentation of the LDS temple. While there he married Maude Fox.

The couple returned to Salt Lake City where Fairbanks entered the University of Utah. At the end of the war he sculpted the *Victorious American Doughboy* for the State of Idaho, then received his first teaching position at the University of Oregon. While there he designed the bronze doors of the United States National Bank in Portland, the ornamentation for St. Mary's Cathedral in Eugene, and a portrait of Ezra Meeker, founder of the Old Oregon Trail Association. In 1924 Fairbanks took a leave of absence to study at Yale University where he earned a Bachelor of Fine Arts Degree. Two years later he received a Guggenheim Fellowship to study in Rome with the Italian sculptor Dante Sodini and in Florence at the Scuola Fiorentina de Pittura. In 1928 he taught at the Seattle Institute of Art, completed a Master of Fine Arts degree at the University of Washington, and began one of his first major statues, the Ninety-First Division

Monument at Fort Lewis, Washington.

Upon completion of his master's degree, Fairbanks accepted a position at the University of Michigan as associate professor and resident sculptor at the newly-formed Institute of Fine Arts. Although in many ways a productive period, because of the Great Depression it was not as fruitful as he hoped. However, he did two of his finest and most original art deco works during this time: *Rain* and *Nebula*. *Rain* was selected for the Brookgreen Sculpture Garden in South Carolina and *Nebula* was exhibited at the 1939 World's Fair in New York.

While living in Michigan Fairbanks continued to keep close ties with his native state. He completed *The Tragedy of Winter Quarters* Memorial for the Pioneer Mormon Cemetery in Omaha, Nebraska, and a portrait bust of LDS president Heber J. Grant. At the university he focused his attention on the study of skeletal and muscular forms, earning a Ph.D. in anatomy in 1936. He also competed energetically for the "Coming of the Pioneers" project.[20] Years later his son Eugene F. Fairbanks reminisced about his father's attempt to win this:

> Avard felt somewhat satisfied that his efforts were recognized and honored when he was chosen as a contestant for the . . . This is the Place Monument. He also realized that there would be [much] . . . to overcome, because Mahonri Young was chosen as the other contestant, and the Young family had considerable political impact.
>
> Avard's concepts of memorials was that they should portray history accurately with [some] drama. He envisioned a great shaft which would support a representative pioneer family coming over a rocky crag with their covered wagon. The monument should be to a great movement, not just a person or small group of men, but to an epic movement of people. In the foreground would be Brigham Young, . . . rising from his carriage, saying "This Is the Place." The structure

DRAWING OF PROPOSED
THIS IS THE PLACE MONUMENT, 1938,
BY AVARD FAIRBANKS
GRAPHITE ON PAPER, 15 1/2″ X 11″
(COURTESY EUGENE F. FAIRBANKS)

would house a history museum below the promenade about the base of the shaft. There would be stairs or an elevator to carry people up to the view terrace about the base of the pioneer family. . . .

The sketch was submitted early in 1938. During that summer the family again drove to Salt Lake City. The competition was to be held in about August. Avard's ambitious plans began to take shape in a scale model which was four feet square at the base and rose to almost four feet at the apex. The courtyard between the studio and home on Whitlock Avenue where John B. Fairbanks resided was a busy place, with brothers, sons, and nephews working together.

While Avard was modeling and casting the sculptured portions of the model, his brother, Ortho, framed up the base and the tower. With the numerous details and the emphasis for perfection, it was taking longer than expected. Avard asked for a couple days extension but was told that if it was not delivered by a three o'clock deadline he would be out of the competition.

The last day was a real hurry up, and the model was loaded on the truck as some of the details and coloring were added. The truck pulled away and arrived at the designated place a few minutes before the deadline.

When he went to meet the committee the next day he was told that the decision had been postponed for six months because Mahonri M. Young had informed them that he had been ill. This was unfortunate for Avard, since he would be teaching sculpture at the University of Michigan . . . [and would find it difficult] to travel to Salt Lake City to present his model and ideas.

He felt some encouragement in that he had two very good friends on the committee who he felt could speak in his behalf. Nothing daunting, when he returned to Ann Arbor, he wrote letters to the chairman and his friends describing his plans. In order to emphasize the quality of his work, he spent many nights in his darkroom enlarging a dozen sets of twelve of his finest monumental sculptures in 11x14 inch prints. These he sent to the committee so that the members could review his masterpieces. Later, he learned that these were never allowed to be shown.

There was not only disappointment but also some bitterness which Avard tried to conceal. He usually said let us not discuss it. Many years later he indicated, when invited to compete for another statue for a western state, that it would be an exercise in futility. Remembering the Mormon Battalion and This is the Place monuments, he said that they must, by law, have a competition, but they probably have already chosen the sculptor. He also said that it was probably a blessing to have lost, considering the politics, problems of funding, and delays which beset Mahonri M. Young.[21]

In January 1939 the committee was ready to make a final decision. They invited both Fairbanks and Young to Salt Lake City to present their models to the full committee. Fairbanks was unable to attend because of university duties in Michigan.

Fairbanks's idea was grand in concept and scale: a massive rectangular shaft, atop of which stood a bronze sculpture of a covered wagon pulled by a team of two oxen with a mounted horse and rider by the side. In the wagon, a mother with child in arms looks toward the man on horseback who leans toward her as if in conversation. A youth drives the oxen. At the base in front of the monument a full-sized Brigham Young, suffering from Rocky Mountain spotted fever, raises up from his bed in Wilford Woodruff's carriage, looks around, and pronounces, "This is the place."

Young's intent was to design an artistically-pleasing as well as historically-accurate memorial.

The focal point was a large central pylon at the top of which stood three figures—Brigham Young, Heber C. Kimball, and Wilford Woodruff, prominent leaders during the pioneer period. Young's decision to portray the Mormon hierarchy rather than the pioneers in general as Fairbanks proposed was a significant choice. Young explained that his intent was symbolic, since, according to accounts, Brigham first viewed the valley from Woodruff's wagon.

Young's design consisted of a large granite base, a central tower, and two arms extending on either side with smaller pylons at the end of each. This symmetrical granite structure provides the backdrop and base for bronze sculptures and reliefs depicting various groups and individual characters important in the state's settlement. Extending across the base is a frieze representing the pioneers. On one pylon is a sculptural group of Spanish fathers and on the other a group of trappers and fur traders. Displayed about the granite base are sculptures in both free-standing groups and sculptural relief, totaling seventy-four human figures.

Presented with both Fairbanks's and Young's proposals, President Grant, the most influential figure on the committee, agreed with Young's intent and told the committee that "they weren't erecting a monument to a covered wagon."[22] Grant's influence proved decisive, as Young was awarded the commission. There is a sense in both Young's and Fairbanks's accounts that a decision had already been made and that Young would get it. Young was elated. Writing to Jack Sears, he said: "This will fittingly memorialize, in an appropriate and substantial manner, the achievements of the Pioneers, who entered the Valley of the Great Salt Lake in 1847 to establish homes and build an inland Empire, and also give full recognition to those trail blazers who had preceded them. I would rather have the This is the Place commission than any other that could come to me."[23] This fulfilled the dream Young had had since first returning from Paris when he believed that the Mormon church would commission monuments to its past.

Young wanted to get started. The model he presented to the committee was small and only roughly indicated the basic shape and what the figures would look like. Besides drawings that Young presented to the committee, the figures and groups were still rough ideas in his head.

The next step was to make detailed scale sculptures in plaster of all the figures. This would allow the artist to finalize his ideas and show the committee exactly what the finished monument would look like. In turn, they could approve or disapprove. This was necessary because changes on a full-scale sculpture would be prohibitive, both in time and money. Although tedious and time-consuming, in many ways this part of the project was the most important in that it determined the final shapes. Afterward the pieces would be enlarged to full size in plaster, then shipped to the foundry where molds would be made and cast in bronze.

The 1939 Utah legislature appropriated only $5,000 for the project. With such a small sum, Young would not be able to complete his design. Determined to persuade the state otherwise, Young took matters into his own hands. At "Utah Day" at the New York World's Fair, Young took Governor Blood to lunch, though nothing came of this. Young was told that a permanent monument committee had been appointed and that things would begin to move ahead. Blood suggested that Young write Grant and Giles, as well as to Clarence Neslen, influential members of the new committee. Young did so without results.[24]

The American Academy in Rome had invited

Young to serve as a professor in residence. Young would be provided with a salary, living quarters, and a large studio. With no teaching duties, he could devote full time and attention to the commission. But to his dismay, with the outbreak of World War II on September 1, 1939, his position abroad was eliminated.

Little progress was made for the remainder of the year. In December Young met with Grant and Neslen during their tour of the church's Eastern States Mission. Grant reassured Young that things would move ahead and that all was well. But nothing happened.

In the spring of 1940, out of sheer frustration, Young wrote to Grant. The monument, he wrote, was not moving ahead because sufficient money was not appropriated to fund the project. Young explained that what progress was made was at his own personal expense.[25]

The artist felt a personal sense of urgency. He had always wanted to sculpt this monument, but advancing age and problems with his health concerned him. He was not sure how many good years he had left. On the occasion of his sixty-third birthday, he wrote, "[N]othing remains but old age and dim shining power. Already I feel the decline. Stooping is an effort and sometimes painful. I can still work several hours a day but I am often very tired at the end of the day."[26]

That same year Young learned that his wife Dorothy had cancer. He was devastated by the news. This was the same disease that had taken his first wife, Cecelia. He wrote, "After my experience in the terrible disease which carried Cecelia off, I do not look forward to the future with much confidence, and after winning the one job I would rather do than any other in the world, I feel that its gain is no more than problematical."[27] Noting that life had taught

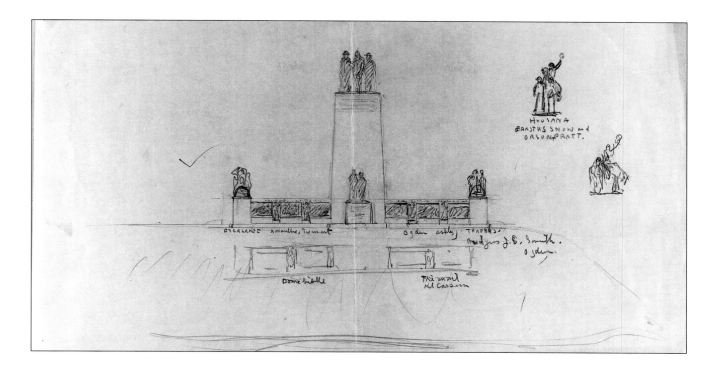

SKETCH FOR THE THIS IS THE PLACE MONUMENT
GRAPHITE ON PAPER, 7″ X 13″
(© COURTESY MUSEUM OF ART, BRIGHAM
YOUNG UNIVERSITY. ALL RIGHTS RESERVED.)

*Young's preliminary sketches for the project show
that even though the basic design of the monument
was altered very little, they do show an interesting
change in concept. In the early stages of the commission it was thought of as a monument to the arrival
of the Mormon pioneers. Later the idea was expanded to portray the discovery and settlement of
Utah in a more general sense. Several preliminary
sketches found in the Young Collection at Brigham
Young University indicate that the monument originally did not include the* Spanish Explorers *and the*
Trappers and Fur Traders Groups. *These sketches
indicate that on each of the smaller pylons, Young
had originally intended to place a large beehive, the
symbol of the Territory of Utah.*

him that little could be gained by worry, he continued to work: "I have never worked harder . . .
and I suppose I have accomplished a lot, but I
do not feel I have accomplished what I should
or could." There was still no formal contract.

In May 1941 Giles sent word that Young
should come to Salt Lake City. But Young was
unable to because he was in the middle of teaching the largest sculpture class in the history of
the Art Students League. The previous February
an article had appeared in *Life* magazine showing
Young teaching at the league.[28] This was good
publicity, but the story concerned the artist
because it contained several embarrassing mis-
quotes and he worried that this might adversely
affect his relationship with the monument committee and leadership of the church. In the article Young was quoted saying that his father was
an apostle in the church and that he had disas-
sociated himself from Mormonism.[29]

Young signed a provisional contract on June

MODEL FOR THE ***Central Group***, PLASTER
THIS IS THE PLACE MONUMENT, (FIRST VERSION)
HEBER C. KIMBALL, BRIGHAM YOUNG, WILFORD WOODRUFF
(PHOTOGRAPHIC ARCHIVES, HAROLD B. LEE LIBRARY,
BRIGHAM YOUNG UNIVERSITY, PROVO, UTAH)

BACK VIEW OF MODEL FOR THE ***Central Group***, PLASTER
THIS IS THE PLACE MONUMENT (FIRST VERSION)
(PHOTOGRAPHIC ARCHIVES, LEE LIBRARY)

28 which stipulated that he would provide and pay for all equipment and materials. It gave him one year to complete a final model which would be subject to the committee's inspection and approval and would become the property of the State of Utah.[30] It provided the artist with $4,000 for this work, an initial payment of $1,000 to be paid on July 12,[31] and the balance divided into four equal installments of $750, the last to be received when the work was completed.

During this time Young's ally Heber J. Grant passed away. His successor as church president was George Albert Smith, who also took charge of the monument committee. This affected Young's relationship with the committee. While enlarging his small original model, Young realized that the central figures of Young, Woodruff, and Kimball presented an aesthetic problem when seen from the rear. From the back there was nothing to relieve the repetition of three pairs of legs which looked to Young "like a row of six stove pipes." A friend suggested that he sculpt a sea gull in flight behind the legs to break up the space. This seemed an excellent solution, but to make this seemingly insignificant change he had to travel to Salt Lake City for approval.

Several committee members objected. This would be out of place in Emigration Canyon, they said, as sea gulls do not fly that far east of the lake. To press his case, Young brought with him a revised model. The committee agreed, provided Young construct a six-foot version and send it to Salt Lake City for final approval, after which it would be shipped back. In light of the sea gull being named Utah's state bird, the objection seemed silly.[32]

With all of this trouble over a sea gull, Young did not receive his final $750 payment until March 21, 1943. Furthermore the state legislature appropriated another $15,000, but it was unavailable until Young could obtain a final contract. It increasingly worried him that he was working without this security. Encouraged in May 1944 when three members of the committee, William H. Reeder, George Q. Morris, and John D. Giles, visited him at his studio in Connecticut, Young commented that Morris seemed particularly sensitive to his feelings and aesthetic considerations. Otherwise the project had become a source of frustration.[33]

After this visit Young was optimistic that a final contract would soon be signed. This was urgent because no progress could be made beforehand and the centennial celebration was now only three years away. But new objections were raised by the committee—challenges to Young's historical accuracy. Samuel Russell complained that Captain Bonneville and Father De Smet may never have set foot in Utah and therefore should be removed.

The most serious objection, however, concerned the representation of Woodruff, one of the three figures atop the central pylon. His clothing was not dignified enough, his descendants complained, especially when compared to Young and Kimball who were dressed in suits while Woodruff wore a shirt and suspendered breeches. Compared to the other figures, they felt he looked like a servant. Young stood by his original representation, insisting that it was historically accurate and that in the case of Young's clothing he had used as a model

MODEL FOR *Central Group*, PLASTER, (FINAL VERSION) THIS IS THE PLACE MONUMENT, HEBER C. KIMBALL, BRIGHAM YOUNG, WILFORD WOODRUFF (PHOTOGRAPHIC ARCHIVES, HAROLD B. LEE LIBRARY, BRIGHAM YOUNG UNIVERSITY, PROVO, UTAH)

a suit actually worn by him. Young made another trip to Salt Lake City to discuss these issues, where he also met with church leaders David McKay and J. Reuben Clark. Finally, at the request of President Smith, Young agreed to make the change.[34]

This necessitated a second provisional contract, signed on August 1, 1944. The state legislature appropriated another $15,000 with the stipulation that the commission would not pay for work performed or materials furnished unless the amount had been approved in writing in advance. Young redid Woodruff in a respectable Prince Albert coat, even though he knew that no one in their right mind would wear such a heavy overcoat in Utah in July.

Despite the changes, Young still did not have the go-ahead. Still he hired Spero Anargyros as an assistant. Anargyros met Young while the former was studying at the Art Students League in the late 1930s. He was on scholarship in the sculpture class of William Zorach and earned money by casting. Through this employment he also became acquainted with Young who taught the school's other sculpture class. When Anargyros learned that the professor had been chosen to do a significant monument, he wanted to become involved. Contrary to his plans, he soon found himself called up for active duty in North Africa when World War II broke out. After returning in the fall of 1944, his first thought was to look up Young who was in Utah. He travelled by bus from Buffalo to Salt Lake City, but he found that Young was "south in some canyon" on a sketching trip. Spero stayed until the older artist returned. While he waited he toured the city, making it a point to visit the Sea Gull Monument, a work that particularly interested him. Young returned so impressed to find his old friend that he promised him the job.

The war was still on when Anargyros began working with Young in Branchville, Connecticut, and he was simultaneously employed in an aircraft production plant in Tareytown, New York. He would work whatever shift was required and then commute thirty-five miles every day to put in another shift for Young. He admitted the difficulty of this arrangement but found the work unusually rewarding.

The final contract was signed at last in November 1945. Young and Anargyros went to Boston, headquarters of the church's Eastern States Mission, where President Smith and other members of the committee participated in the signing.[35]

Now Young faced other difficulties. Because the civilian work force was directed toward the war effort, there was a shortage of manpower. In addition, cold weather, bad road conditions, and the fact that Young was sixty-eight years old caused innumerable, unavoidable delays.

As the dedication drew near, personal tragedy struck. Dorothy, who earlier had been diagnosed with cancer, became seriously ill in April. Exploratory surgery at a New York City hospital revealed that the disease had spread throughout her stomach and that nothing could be done. Her condition continued to worsen. On June 22 doctors told Mahonri that his wife did not have long to live. The next day he took a train from their home in Connecticut to New York. She passed away later that day. Young had hoped that she would be with him at the dedication of the monument, and her death left a void that was inconsolable.[36] Perhaps as a premonition he had inscribed her initials D. W. on the yoke of the oxen in the *Donner Party* relief.

It was good that Young had the pressure of finishing the monument within just one year to keep his mind off of this personal loss. Completion of the monument would go right down to the wire. On July 5, 1947, the *Central Group* would be lifted into place atop the sixty-foot pylon, but all the bronzes had not yet arrived from the foundry in Brooklyn, New York. Still undelivered were the trapper group and the six figures for the east side of the monument.

The major sculptural pieces and groups of the monument are signed and dated, indicating the order in which Young finished them. The first to be completed was the *Donner Party* relief, dated 1945. The next year, in 1946, he completed the reliefs of Orson Pratt and Erastus Snow and the *Wagon Train* frieze, the *Spanish Explorers: Father Escalante and Dominguez Group*, and the *Trappers and Fur Traders*

Group. Finally in 1947 he completed the six single figures on the back of the monument. This includes *Washakie*, inscribed with the following: "Mahonri Feb. 26, 1947 FINIS."

As with every phase of the commission, dedication day was not without its own frustrations. The bronze descriptive plaques with historical background describing the figures were not yet mounted and were supported by wooden stakes. This looked unsightly to the artist who wanted them laid flat so they would not detract from the lines of the monument. Despite his wishes, the plaques were left up. Later when they were permanently installed, Young wanted them mounted upright, but Giles wanted them laid flat. Young felt that Giles did this to spite him, another incident in the rift between the two men.[37]

Young said that the centennial celebration was "the greatest day of my life," but it was also the culmination of his greatest trial—nor did the artist's troubles end on July 24, 1947. Although he had completed the monument, he would still have to deal with the Monument Commission Committee for almost two more years. Not until then did he receive final payment, which he felt cheated him by $11,000.

The long delay in payment was caused by a law suit involving the general contractor of the granite portion, one of the five major contractors involved in constructing the monument. Five months after the dedication, the granite base was still not finished and the services of contractor Daniel McCarthy were terminated.

Otto Beuhner and Co. was hired to complete the work and redo parts of the monument that were unsatisfactory. McCarthy filed suit against the State of Utah, the monument commission, and ten members of the committee for a total of $42,000. The monument commission countersued for $61,000. In 1948 a court granted McCarthy $4,000.[38]

When Young finally received his last payment, the bank refused to cash the check because of a missing signature. Young sent the check back to Giles, special delivery, with a bank statement explaining why they could not cash it, along with a personal letter. Giles never responded. A month later, in a letter dated February 11, 1949, Young asked Jack Sears if he would contact Giles and as tactfully as possible see what he could do to get the missing signature. With Sears's help Young was able to cash the check.[39]

Because of the wording of the final contract, payments promised Young under the provisional contracts were never paid. Acknowledging the le-gality of what the committee had drafted, Young felt they had intentionally cheated him in the way the document was written up. When he realized what had occurred, he wrote to the committee expressing his grievances. He considered writing to President Smith who was seriously ill. Young was reluctant, but, as time went on and the committee did nothing, he finally wrote to the church president. This precipitated a severe rebuke from George Morris who instructed Young never to write Smith again about such matters. To the end of his life Young never forgave the commission. He wrote bitterly that he was sadder but wiser.[40]

Wayne Hinton, the first to thoroughly research the documents concerning this matter, concluded that "Young's contentions were not entirely a sour grapes matter."[41] Besides denying him the $11,000 for his preliminary work, the fact that Young did not receive final payment until nearly two years after the monument was dedicated had only added insult to injury. The irony is that the monument was meant to celebrate a heritage of integrity,

Central Group, THIS IS THE PLACE MONUMENT AT THE FOUNDRY, C. E. HALBACK AND CO., BROOKLYN, NEW YORK (PHOTOGRAPHIC ARCHIVES, HAROLD B. LEE LIBRARY, BRIGHAM YOUNG UNIVERSITY, PROVO, UTAH.)

honesty, and hard work, yet the circumstances surrounding its building were fraught with pettiness and legal arm-wrestling.

Within two weeks of the monument's dedication Young's turned seventy. He knew that he did not have many productive years left and that this just might be the culmination of his artistic career. Seen in that light, the monument aptly sums up his life's work.

From the very beginning Young's concept was to create a visual history of the Mormon trek. At the start there is some indication that he intended to include only the Mormon story. One of his early drawings shows monumental beehives, the symbol of the former State of Deseret and the present State of Utah, on the north and south pylons. In

subsequent drawings the beehives were replaced by the Spanish explorers and the trappers and traders. As the commission progressed and state funds began to be involved, committee members felt that the monument should not be limited to the Mormon era. Young may have drawn his own inspiration from B. H. Roberts's six-volume *A Comprehensive History of the Church* which is dominated by the story of Mormonism but also includes the histories of those who came before.[42] In a chapter entitled "The Salt Lake Valley Before the Advent of the 'Mormon' Pioneers," the first two subheadings are "Roman Catholic Fathers in Utah Lake Valley—1776" and "The Hunter and Trapper Period."

The central tower is over sixty feet tall, on top of which stand three figures, each over eighteen feet in height. Here are depicted the principal Mormon leaders at the time of the great exodus. Brigham Young stands in the center with a cane in his right hand. Wilford Woodruff stands on his left, Heber C. Kimball on his right. Kimball holds a whip in his right hand and a hat in his left. Woodruff stands with his left arm outstretched as if to steady Young. Just below, carved in the granite base, are Brigham's famous words, "This is the Place." All the lettering for the monument was done by the artist's life-long friend Waldo Midgley.

Designed to be viewed from a distance, the three central figures are boldly and simply modeled. Standing so far above ground level, they, in fact, cannot be viewed up close. Here Young's skill and mastery are evident, for they are successful likenesses from far off.

On the lower west front at the base of the central pylon are over-life-sized images of Orson Pratt and Erastus Snow represented in silhouetted bronze high relief against the granite background. On July 21 Pratt and Snow were the first from the company to see the Salt Lake Valley. In their excitement they waved their hats above their heads and shouted, "Hosannah!" With only one horse between them, they then made their way into the valley and spent the rest of the day exploring. In this sculpture Young captured the moment when they first saw the valley. One figure standing, the other on horseback, they wave their hats and shout. Below them in granite are carved the words, "Hosannah, Hosannah, Hosannah," followed by a passage from Isaiah that the pioneers felt was prophetic of their accomplishment: "And it shall come to pass that in the last days that the mountain of the Lord's house shall be established in the top of the mountains and shall be exalted above the hills and all nations shall flow unto it. The wilderness and the desert shall rejoice and blossom as a rose."

Artistically the finest work of the entire monument is the *Donner Party* relief. This beautiful piece, reminiscent of the Sea Gull Monument, shows the dynamism, poetry, and power of Young's sculpture at its best. This large relief is on the back, or east side, of the central pylon. Here Young pays tribute to the pioneer company that preceded the Mormon exodus, clearing the trail into the Salt Lake Valley on their way to California. The Donner Party works their way through Emigration Canyon blazing the trail that Mormons would follow the next year. Apart from the disaster that befell them in the Sierra Nevadas, this was the most strenuous and critical part of their entire trip. The going was so difficult that they literally exhausted themselves

Central Group, This is the Place Monument: Heber C. Kimball, Brigham Young, and Wilford Woodruff bronze, monumental (18')

This is the Place Monument, This is the Place State Park, Salt Lake City, Utah photo by Craig Law.

Hosannah Shout, 1946-47
ORSON PRATT AND ERASTUS SNOW

BRONZE, MONUMENTAL
THIS IS THE PLACE MONUMENT,
THIS IS THE PLACE STATE PARK,
SALT LAKE CITY, UTAH
PHOTO BY CRAIG LAW.

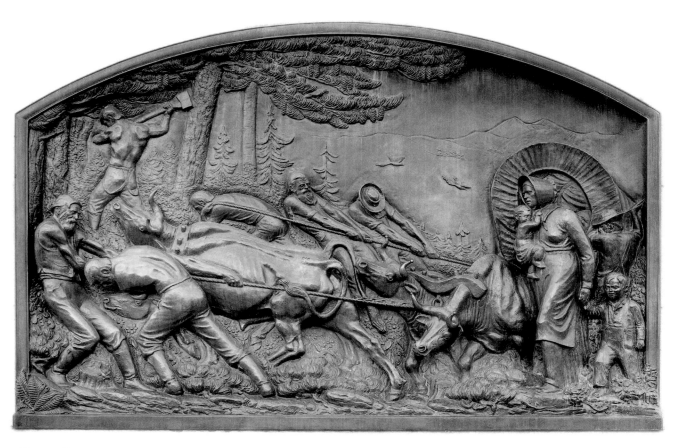

Donner Party RELIEF, 1945-47
BRONZE, 82″ X 124″
THIS IS THE PLACE MONUMENT,
THIS IS THE PLACE STATE PARK,
SALT LAKE CITY, UTAH
PHOTO BY CRAIG LAW.

Wagon Train FRIEZE, NORTH ARM, 1946-47, BRONZE
THIS IS THE PLACE MONUMENT, THIS IS THE PLACE STATE PARK,
SALT LAKE CITY, UTAH. PHOTO BY CRAIG LAW.

and their animals and lost critical time that made the difference between getting through the Sierra Nevadas safely and getting caught by early winter storms.

Preparatory drawings show that from the beginning Young knew what he intended to portray with this group. He borrowed from figures and themes he had explored earlier. The power and energy of the pioneer men are reminiscent of his early laborers. The man wielding an axe in the upper left is comparable to *Man with a Pick* or *Man with a Heavy Sledge*. In the lower left the figure of the woman wearing a bonnet, hand in hand with a child at her side, is similar to the artist's sculpture for the Pioneer Woman Memorial, as well as to figures from the Sea Gull Monument. Again the Sea Gull Monument comes to mind in terms of the beauty

and skill Young demonstrated in his mastery of relief sculpture. This work is rich in detail and shows the historical as well as physical accuracy characteristic of his work. Small lizards scurry about on the rocks in the foreground, while in the sky above several magpies fly by.

Facing north and south on the monument is a group of figures in silhouette: riders on horseback representing the nine men who entered the Salt Lake Valley one day after Snow and Pratt. Four appear on the north side, five on the south. Individual figures are reminiscent of previous small bronzes Young executed of the *Pioneer* and *The Frontiersman*. The poses and positions create a dynamic sense of movement and flow.

Across the base of the monument facing west, on arms that connect the smaller north-south

Wagon Train FRIEZE, SOUTH ARM, 1946-47, BRONZE
THIS IS THE PLACE MONUMENT, THIS IS THE PLACE STATE PARK,
SALT LAKE CITY, UTAH. PHOTO BY CRAIG LAW.

pylons, Young sculpted a large bronze frieze representing the main wagon train of the first pioneer company. The figures in the frieze move from south to north. The north side represents the main group that entered on July 23, while the south half depicts the last group from the company making their way into the valley about noon on July 24, 1847. Here again can be seen Young's attention to history. In the north group the figures are only men, while in the south group are three women and two children who were part of the pioneer company. On the south section of the frieze, Brigham rides in Woodruff's carriage, sick with mountain fever. He lifts himself up on one arm at the moment when he is said to have remarked, "This is the place, drive on."

For this artist, this must have been the most personal part of the monument. Here he portrays his grandfather, Brigham Young, with his wife Clara Decker Young, who had raised Mahonri's father. Mahonri used his own grandson Charles as the model for the boy with his dog in the foreground. Counting Mahonri himself as the creator of this work, the artist symbolically represented four generations of Youngs.

These two friezes demonstrate Mahonri's technical mastery of bronze sculpture. Because of their size, one continuous piece could not be cast. Young had to take into account the difference in the expansion and contraction of the granite base and the bronze frieze during seasonal and weather changes. The sculptor solved this problem by dividing each side of the frieze into three sections so that each piece would slide under and fit into the next one,

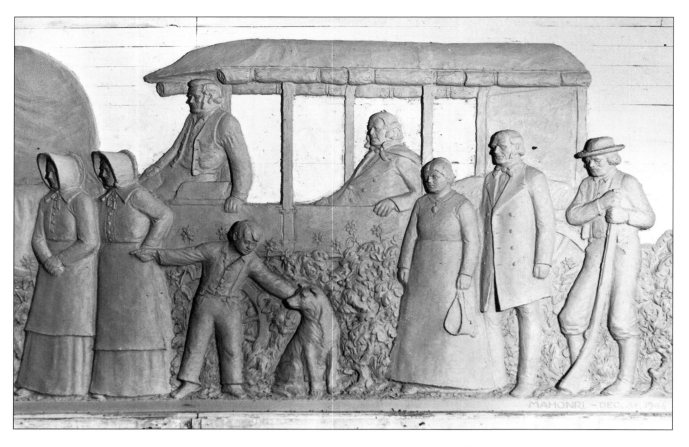

allowing the stone and bronze to expand and contract without buckling. His divisions are so well executed that they are not noticeable unless one looks for them specifically.

On the east face the artist sculpted six individual figures of men prominent in the exploration, discovery, and settlement of Utah. To the south, from left to right, appear *Etienne Provost*, Shoshone chief *Washakie*, and *Peter Skene Ogden*, while to the north, from left to right, are *Captain Bonneville*, *Father De Smet*, and *John C. Fremont*.

Provost was sent by the Rocky Mountain Fur Company to explore the Great Basin region. In 1824 he entered the valley south of the Great Salt

Lake. The river he found there still bears his name.

Washakie, a major local Indian leader at the time the Mormons settled the region, was alternately sympathetic and hostile toward anglos. In Young's portrayal of the Native American chief, he honors the people who originally settled the land.

Ogden was among the most important trappers of the Hudson Bay Company. In the 1820s he trapped on the Bear River in Cache Valley as well as other areas, including what is now known as the Ogden area.

Captain Benjamin Louis Eulalie de Bonneville, on leave from the army to explore, entered the Green River Valley in 1832 with 110 trappers. He

Captain Bonneville, Father De Smet,
AND ***John C. Fremont***, 1946-47

BRONZE, MONUMENTAL
THIS IS THE PLACE MONUMENT, THIS IS THE PLACE
STATE PARK, SALT LAKE CITY, UTAH. PHOTO BY CRAIG LAW.

sent forty men south to the Salt Lake Valley.
Bonneville may never have set foot in Utah, but
his name is associated with the region. In 1837 he
produced a map that gave the salt inland lake his
name. It was later changed, but the ancient lake,
of which the Great Salt Lake is a remnant, is still
known as Lake Bonneville.

Father Pierre-Jean De Smet, another explorer,
passed through the valley in 1841. Five years later,
while on the Missouri frontier, he met Brigham
Young near Omaha where he gave a favorable account of what he had seen in the Great Basin.

Colonel John C. Fremont was one of the great
explorers of the Rocky Mountain region and the

Pacific Coast. While on his second trip west in
1843 he wrote the first accurate description of the
Great Basin. His topographical map of the area was
published in 1845, upon which the Mormons relied
extensively.

These six figures were the last Young did in his
rush to complete the monument on schedule.
Though historically accurate and stately in pose,
compared with other parts of the monument they
seem to lack a sense of refinement and finish that
appear elsewhere.

The two smaller pylons support the *Spanish
Explorers: Fathers Escalante and Dominguez Group*
and the *Trappers and Fur Traders Group*. Each

Etienne Provost, Washakie, AND ***Peter Skene Ogden***, 1946-47

BRONZE, MONUMENTAL. THIS IS THE PLACE MONUMENT, THIS IS THE PLACE STATE PARK, SALT LAKE CITY, UTAH. PHOTO BY CRAIG LAW

Trappers and Fur Traders Group, 1946-47

BRONZE, MONUMENTAL. THIS IS THE PLACE MONUMENT
PHOTO BY CRAIG LAW

Spanish Explorers: Fathers Escalante and Dominguez Group, 1946-47
BRONZE, MONUMENTAL. THIS IS THE PLACE MONUMENT, THIS IS THE PLACE STATE PARK,
SALT LAKE CITY, UTAH. PHOTO BY CRAIG LAW

group has a mounted central figure. Both are similar in composition, which adds to the symmetry of the monument.

Roman Catholic priests were the first Europeans to set foot in Utah. In 1776 a group of ten fathers set out from Santa Fe in search of an overland route to Monterey, California. Their explorations were recorded by Father Francisco Escalante who, mounted on a burro, is the central figure in the *Spanish Explorers Group*. Their leader, Francisco Atanario Dominguez, leads the burro while the rest of the group follow on foot. The other figures repre-

sented are Don Juan Pedro Oiseros, Don Bernardo Miera y Pacheco, Don Joaquin Lain, Lorenzo Olivares, Lucrecio Muniz, Andres Muniz, Juan de Aguilare, and Simon Luceros. Young used the same habit for his model that he had formerly used in the Father Kino Memorial.

On the north pylon is the group representing the trappers and traders. These were the men from the great fur companies who first explored the intermountain region. Because he was the first to explore the region, William H. Ashley is mounted on horseback and surrounded by Jedediah S.

Smith, James (Jim) Bridger, Thomas (Broken Hand) Fitzpatrick, Robert Campbell, David E. Jackson, William L. and Milton Sublette, and Hugh Glass. They occupy the north pylon because they came from the north. Earlier works by Young, such as the *Frontiersman*, are similar to any one of the figures of the *Trappers and Fur Traders Group*.

The This is the Place Monument as a whole is dominated by a feeling of monumentality and classical restraint. Young's intent, besides providing an aesthetically satisfying memorial, was to be historically thorough. Because of its size, one can only view the monument up close in sections, causing some observers to comment: "[I]t always seems more a book to be read than something aesthetically dynamic in its unity. Including a number of admirable passages in regards to Young's gift for energetic portrayal, the sum doesn't measure up to the parts."[43] As a landmark, the monument is nevertheless one of the most enduring symbols of Utah, second only to the Mormon temple as a widely-recognized site with a clear message. It is unfortunate that its massive scale hampers appreciation of the many finely-crafted bronze details. But this was not the artist's intent. It is a monument to a Hegira, not to an artist. Still if one looks closely, one sees in the graceful, powerful lines the evidence of a master's hand.

In size alone, this is one of the great monuments commemorating the American West. In particular it pays tribute to the story of the Mormons and to the land they settled, a detailed and complex story brought together in grand style. To stand behind the This is the Place Monument with the sun setting into the mountains west of the Great Salt Lake is a memorable experience, one that brings to mind the epochal nature of this remarkable story, mirrored in the artist's own life and accomplishments.

Notes

1. Wallace Stegner, *The Gathering of Zion: The Story of the Mormon Trail* (Lincoln: University of Nebraska Press, 1981), 1-2.

2. *Deseret News*, July 24, 1849; B. H. Roberts, *Comprehensive History of the Church of Jesus Christ of Latter-day Saints*, 6 vols. (Provo, UT: Brigham Young University Press, 1965), 3:493-97.

3. Davis Bitton, "The Ritualization of Mormon History," *Utah Historical Quarterly* 43 (Winter 1975): 72. A detailed description of the procession and program is in the *Deseret News*, July 28, 1880. See also *The Utah Pioneers: Celebration of the Entrance of the Pioneers into Great Salt Lake Valley* (Salt Lake City, 1880).

4. Stegner, 168.

5. Milton W. Brown et al., *American Art: Painting, Sculpture, Architecture, Decorative Arts, Photography* (New York: Prentice Hall, Inc., Harry N. Abrams, 1979), 563.

6. Young to Jack Sears, Jack Sears Collection, Mss. 1058, box 3, folder 5, Archives and Manuscripts, Harold B. Lee Library, Brigham Young University, Provo, Utah.

7. Grant to Young, July 21, 1920, Mahonri Young Collection, Mss. 4, box 3, Archives and Manuscripts, Lee Library.

8. "This is the Place Monument Commission," A Report to Governor Blood and the Twenty-Third Legislative Assembly of Utah, 4-5.

9. Ibid.

10. *Deseret News,* July 16, 1934.

11. Young, "This is the Place Monument," box 7, folder 17.

12. Quoted in Mahonri Young to Bill Young, July 22, 1936, box 3.

13. Young, "This is the Place Monument."

14. Mahonri Young to Jack Sears, Feb. 17, 1937, box 3, folder 5, Sears Collection.

15. "This is the Place Monument" folder, archives, Historical Department, Church of Jesus Christ of Latter-day Saints, Salt Lake City, Utah.

16. Young to Jack Sears, Feb. 8, 1938, box 3, folder 5, Sears Collection.

17. Ibid.

18. Young to Jack Sears, Aug. 21, 1939, box 3, folder 5, Sears Collection.

19. *New York Herald*, Dec. 2, 1910.

20. Eugene F. Fairbanks, "A Sculptor's Testimony in Bronze and Stone: The Sacred Sculpture of Avard T. Fairbanks," *Avard T. Fairbanks: Eight Decades. A Retrospective Exhibition* (Provo, UT: Brigham Young University, 1987).

21. Personal remembrance of Eugene F. Fairbanks, dated May 10, 1989, copy in my possession. I appreciate Dr. Fairbanks's permission to publish this.

22. Young, "This is the Place Monument."

23. Young to Sears, Mar. 30, 1939, box 3, Sears Collection.

24. See Wayne Kendall Hinton, "A Biographical History of Mahonri M. Young, A Western American Artist," Ph.D. diss., Brigham Young University, 1974, 205.

25. Young to Sears, Mar. 30, 1939.

26. Mahonri Young, Journal, box 3, folder 9.

27. Ibid.

28. "Mahonri Young's Sculpture Preserves His Mormon Past," *Life*, Feb. 17, 1941, 76-79.

29. Ibid.; also Young to Jack Sears, Mar. 1941, box 3, Sears Collection.

30. "This is the Place Monument" folder, LDS church archives.

31. *The Salt Lake Tribune*, July 12, 1941.

32. Young, "This is the Place Monument."

33. Young to Jack Sears, May 19, 1944, box 3, Sears Collection.

34. Young, "This is the Place Monument."

35. Ibid.

36. Young to Jack Sears, May 20 and June 23, 1947, box 3, Sears Collection.

37. Young, "This is the Place Monument."

38. "This is the Place Monument" folder, LDS church archives

39. Young to Jack Sears, Feb. 11, 1949, box 3, Sears Collection.

40. Young, "This is the Place Monument"; compare Young to Jack Sears, Nov. 25, 1945, box 3, Sears Collection.

41. See Hinton, 219-20, for a thoroughly documented discussion.

42. Roberts, *Comprehensive History of the Church*, 3:245-67, Chapter LXXXI, "The Salt Lake Region Before the Advent of the 'Mormon' Pioneers." Roberts's history was first published between 1892 and 1915.

43. Robert Olpin, *Dictionary of Utah Art* (Salt Lake City: Salt Lake Art Center, 1980), 292.

CHAPTER 10.

Final Years

Kicked out in old age at last.

—Mahonri Young

It is fitting that the last major commission of Mahonri Young's career was a statue of his grandfather. All his life he had wanted to sculpt a memorial to Brigham Young, and for years he had collected pictures in hopes that some day he would have the opportunity.[1] The chance came when the State of Utah proposed placing a statue of its first territorial governor in Statuary Hall in the United States Capitol.

Statuary Hall had been in existence for almost one hundred years. In 1853, after the capitol was enlarged with new House and Senate wings, Congress debated what to do with the soon-to-be-vacated Old House Chambers. It was thought that the space could be used to display historical paintings, but the room's semi-circular shape and columned walls were not suitable. It was then suggested that the area might be better suited for sculpture, but no action was taken. After the House of Representatives moved into its new quarters in 1857, the vacant auditorium became a cluttered thoroughfare between the rotunda and the House wing.

Finally, on July 2, 1864, a resolution was passed and the Old House Chambers officially became the National Statuary Hall: "[T]he President is hereby authorized to invite each and every State to provide and furnish statues, in marble or bronze, not exceeding two in number from each State, of deceased persons who have been citizens thereof, and illustrious for their historic renown or for distinguished civic or military service such as each State may deem to be worthy of this national commemoration."[2]

By 1933 the hall contained so many pieces that the Capitol architect expressed concern that the floor would not hold the weight. At the time Utah was not yet represented at all and already sixty-five marble and bronze statues crowded the hall, three deep in some places. Since each state was allowed to display two works, more were forthcoming. It was decided to limit the number of statues in the hall to forty-eight, one from each state. The remainder would be placed on display in other areas in the Capitol.[3]

When the State of Utah first proposed a

Brigham Young statue in the 1940s, Mahonri was bringing the This is the Place Monument to completion. He was not the only artist interested in the project. Again Avard Fairbanks was his main competitor, though many of those who would decide thought it appropriate that a grandson should be the sculptor. Nevertheless one of the committee's major concerns was that Mahonri was so old and in such poor health that his ability to complete the project was doubtful. He was now in his seventies, and his health and age were factors that could not be overlooked. Even lifelong friend Lee Richards believed that he would never live to see the statue finished. But Mahonri wanted the commission very much. It was a desire born out of the pride and the deep respect he had always felt for his grandfather. Furthermore the statue would be displayed in a prestigious setting, and in the artist's mind age would not be a deterrent to such a calling.

Despite the concerns, Young set out to do all he could to secure the commission. He began by asking Jack Sears to help gain support for him in Utah while he went to Washington, D.C., to meet with Utah's senators. As a result of his vigorous campaign, the question about his health was allayed. The final decision, however, would not be made by the committee. To honor the wishes of the Young family, especially the living children, the committee and the state decided to leave the selection to the family.

Mahonri immediately set out to win support of Brigham's three living daughters, knowing that their main concern would be how their father's demeanor would be portrayed. More than anything else they wanted the sculpture to emphasize his gentle, domestic nature as a father and family man. Family members had criticized Cyrus Dallin's statue because of the severe facial expression.

More than once they had expressed their displeasure to Mahonri at family gatherings. Mahonri understood and was sympathetic to Dallin's intent, as he too wanted to depict the great leader and colonizer as the "Lion of the Lord, the Rock of Granite, the Old Man of the Mountain."[4] Ingeniously he devised a solution to the problem that he hoped would please both himself and the family. In a preliminary study he modeled a small statuette of the leader seated. Giving one side of the face a stern expression while modeling the other with a more pleasant demeanor, he blended the two expressions in the middle. On the left side of the face Mahonri raised the corner of the mouth to create a pleasant, almost smiling expression, while on the right the mouth is lowered, giving that side a stern expression.[5]

He attended the Young family reunion on June 1, 1944, and presented his statuette to the family. He later described what transpired in letters to friends. The oldest daughter, Mabel, reiterated that she did not want her father depicted as in Dallin's statue. Mahonri took this as his cue. As she frowned, he asked her to keep her eyes on the model while he slowly turned it so she could see the profile of the other side. When the left side came into view, she smiled. This was what she wanted. It represented the kindly side of Brigham.[6]

Won over by this demonstration, the family had another objection. The artist depicted his grandfather with a long beard, but the family remembered that in later years his beard was short. Mahonri preferred the longer growth for artistic reasons. Visually it connected the head with the body and enhanced the dignity of the figure. He knew that artistic considerations alone would not influence the family, so he told them that he used the beard to hide Brigham's goiter. This proved satisfactory.[7]

Mahonri Young in his studio, ca. 1947

(Photographic Archives, Harold B. Lee Library,
Brigham Young University, Provo, Utah)

Brigham Young STATUE, 1950
MARBLE, 5′ 11″ HIGH, NATIONAL STATUARY HALL,
UNITED STATES CAPITOL, WASHINGTON, D.C.
(PHOTO, MUSEUM OF CHURCH HISTORY AND
ART, THE CHURCH OF JESUS CHRIST OF
LATTER-DAY SAINTS, SALT LAKE CITY, UTAH)

This, he said, is why he chose to depict him as elder statesman in a socratic pose. When he presented his case to the committee, he also pointed out that no known photographs existed of Brigham in his later years standing. The committee conceded.[8]

As soon as Young was awarded the commission, he continued to research his subject so that the final marble would be as close a likeness and as historically accurate as possible. Two photographs were particularly helpful, a profile and a picture of the back of the head taken at the request of Brigham's son John W. Young, knowing that someday an artist would find the angles useful. In addition Mahonri traveled to Washington, D.C., to study the surroundings where the statue would be placed. There he paid special attention to the architecture and lighting, took measurements, and obsered the placement of the statues already there.

In 1947, after extensive preliminary work, Young completed a full-scale model which he had cast in plaster and shipped to Utah for public display in the lobby of the Hotel Utah during the Pioneer Day celebration and the unveiling of the This is the Place Monument. The work was well received. However, the stress and strain of the This is the Place Monument took a toll on Young's health. After the dedication he went on vacation to Arizona to revisit Hopi and Navajo country. Returning to Salt Lake City he complained of chest pains and was diagnosed with a mild heart attack. From this time on his mobility was somewhat inhibited. Nevertheless he turned his attention to the final marble statue.

The State of Utah had appropriated $20,000 for the project, $5,000 for committee expenses and for the dedication ceremony and $15,000 for

Although Mahonri's seated figure won the approval of the family, some committee members wanted a full-length standing statue. The artist felt that he might be accused of replicating Dallin's work or that it might too closely resemble his own representation in the This is the Place Monument. He told the committee he wanted to sculpt Brigham as he appeared late in life, arguing that as he grew older and more feeble he preferred to ride rather than walk, sit rather than stand.

the artist. Young estimated that a block of Italian Cararra marble would cost $1,200, while a comparable block of Vermont marble would cost $12,500, so he decided to do the actual carving in Italy, "the cradle of art," and shipped the plaster cast to Italy.

This scheme was not without its complications. For various reasons Young's voyage was delayed, and, after his arrival, finding an adequate block of marble proved more difficult than he had expected. Bombing during World War II had damaged the quarry, making a large block of stone without cracks or fissures almost impossible to find. Very thin cracks are often undetectable until carving actually commences. A minor flaw can develop into a major difficulty and any weakness can cause the finished sculpture to break when transported.[9]

Young finally found what seemed to be a suitable block, but as he began to carve he discovered a major fault running diagonally across the chest area. This rendered the stone useless, and Young had to spend four months locating another piece. When he began again to carve, he found this block too hard. The work went so slowly and the carving proved so difficult that in sheer frustration he gave up and set out to find a third block, though the cumulative cost was far more than he had estimated. Nevertheless the three blocks were still less costly than Vermont marble, so he proceeded with his plans. He finally completed the *Brigham Young* statue on June 1, 1949, after which it was crated and made ready for shipment.

As had been the case with most of the commissions in Young's career, a conflict arose, this time over placement of the work. The artist's study of the lighting convinced him that his work should be placed by a rotunda window. However, the Joint Legislative Commission of the State of Utah wanted it placed in the main circle with the

MAHONRI YOUNG WITH THE
Brigham Young STATUE, 1950
(PHOTOGRAPHIC ARCHIVES, HAROLD B. LEE LIBRARY,
BRIGHAM YOUNG UIVERSITY, PROVO, UTAH)

important statues. Again Young fought tenaciously for his point of view, but in the end the monument was placed in the circle. In compromise, Brigham was placed between Alexander Stephens and Ethan Allen to be a little closer to a window.

Church and government leaders attended the unveiling ceremony on June 2, 1950, the anniversary of Brigham Young's birth. Governor J. Bracken Lee of Utah presented the statue, which was accepted on behalf of Congress by Senator Carl Haydon of Arizona. Orson Whitney Young, a great-grandson; Mahonri Young, a grandson; and Mabel Young Sandborn, the last living child of Brigham Young, unveiled the statue.

One of few seated statues, *Brigham Young* is stately and simple with a monumental grandeur

Brigham Young STATUE
RIGHT SIDE (DETAIL)
(PHOTOGRAPHIC ARCHIVES, HAROLD B. LEE LIBRARY,
BRIGHAM YOUNG UNIVERSITY, PROVO, UTAH)

Brigham Young STATUE
LEFT SIDE (DETAIL)

similar to the feeling Daniel Chester French captured in his Lincoln Memorial. In many ways
Brigham was to the Mormons what Lincoln was
to the country, one who saw his people through
hard times. Mahonri's statue depicts Brigham in
a dignified pose, one hand grasping the arm of his
chair while the other rests in his lap. The chair
itself is significant as lion heads are carved at the
ends of the arms, a symbolic reference to
Brigham's epithet. This may have further significance as the symbol of Solomon who was known
for his wisdom. At the point where the front legs
of the chair meet the seat, small beehives adorn
the chair—the symbol of the territory Brigham
colonized and governed, the Territory of Deseret

and later the State of Utah, "the Beehive State."
The spirit of this work, by Brigham Young's grand-
son, may be summed up in the words of Jedediah
M. Grant, in an 1853 letter to the editor of the
New York Herald:

> I can't undertake to explain Brigham Young to
> your Atlantic citizens, or expect you to put him
> at his value. Your great men Eastward are to
> me like your ivory and pearl handled table
> knives, balance handles, more shiny than the
> inside of my watch case; but, with only edge
> enough to slice bread and cheese or help spoon
> victuals, and all alike by the dozen one with an-
> other. Brigham is the article that sells out West
> with us—between a Roman cutlass and a beef
> butcher knife, the thing to cut up a deer or cut

down an enemy, and that will save your life or carve your dinner every bit as well, though the handpiece is buck horn and the case a hog-skin hanging in the breech of your pantaloons. You, that judge men by the handle and sheath, how can I make you know a good *Blade?*[10]

With this last major work, a fitting climax to a long and productive career, Mahonri considered himself retired. By now age affected him. Up to this time he had been a juror for art shows but even this ceased. He juried his last show in March 1950. After that he did almost no new work. Rather than starting new projects he finished those in progress. He continued to make prints and said that etching gave him great pleasure.

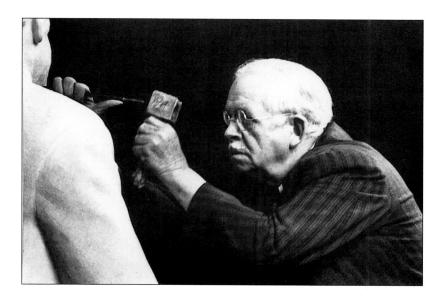

The artist, 1950
(Mahonri Young Collection
Special Collections and Manuscripts,
Photographic Archives, Harold B. Lee Library,
Brigham Young University, Provo, Utah)

With ever-increasing medical bills he made a concerted effort to sell his work. Over the years he had gathered paintings, drawings, prints, and sculptures that he had not attempted to market. Jack and Florence Sears represented him in the West. Florence, he said, sold more of his works than anyone. In the East he was represented by the Kraushaar Galleries in Manhattan, among other dealers.

A year after the *Brigham Young* statue was dedicated, in July 1951, Young fell down some stairs. Fortunately he suffered only bruises, but his neck was so sore that he couldn't work for some time. He began to experience problems with his ankles that made walking difficult. His doctor told him to lose weight. At the same time Young began to have stomach problems and spent his seventy-seventh birthday in the hospital suffering from ulcers. In June 1955 he was back in the hospital with ulcers. He had lost close to fifty pounds but

was so discouraged that he referred to his frequent hospitalizations as incarcerations. In March 1956 he suffered from phlebitis and again had to be hospitalized. That same year he completed his final commission, a commemorative relief sculpture of his friend Victor McCutchen for the Gunnery School in Washington, D.C. In earlier years this small project would have taken him a short time, but between illness and hospitalization it took two years to finish. This, he said, was the hardest work he ever did and he was greatly relieved when it was done.

To the end of his life Mahonri Young never lost his sense of humor, nor his will.

Young wrote to Jack Sears that he wished he had enough energy for one last good fight with John Giles and the This is the Place Monument Commission. They had recently appropriated $20,000 to lay the bronze inscriptions flat, which,

Mahonri believed, would render them illegible. In old age he often joked about the human condition. In 1954 he penned the following:

Kicked out in old age at last,
Like an old horse, to grass;
To graze on the barren hillside
Where pass children on their way to school;
Worn out, and like a much used tool,
Whose use had gone,
Whose edge no longer cuts,
As once it used
When blade and edge were shiny bright
And all was well and life was right:
But now how different are the days
Dredge as we will,
The future holds no light
Whereby we may steer our course,
But never sinks the slope.
To what abyss?

What matters it?
Downward we trend—
Losses now are all our added years.
No more we count the birthdays
As they pass but with sad and numbing hearts
Contemplate with cold dread the diminishing
       future.[11]

In January 1957 Young suffered a serious stroke that left him almost incapacitated. Even though his spirits seemed high, it was obvious to friends and family that he would not work again. On October 5 he suffered an acute ulcer attack which proved to be his final illness. On November 2, at eighty years of age, he passed away, the result of a bleeding ulcer complicated by pneumonia.[12] He was laid to rest in the Young family plot next to Cecelia in Salt Lake City.

Notes

1. Mahonri Young to Bill Patrick, June 1, 1949, Mahonri Young Collection, Mss. 4, box 3, folder 6, Archives and Manuscripts, Harold B. Lee Library, Brigham Young University, Provo, Utah.

2. *Art in the United States Capitol* (Washington, D.C.: U.S. Government Printing Office, 1976), 219.

3. Ibid.

4. Young to Bill Patrick, June 1, 1949.

5. Young to Jack Sears, May 19, 1944, Jack Sears Collection, Mss. 1058, box 3, Archives and Manuscripts, Lee Library.

6. Young to Bill Patrick, June 1, 1949.

7. Ibid.

8. Ibid.

9. Young, "Barrow, George," box 5, folder 9.

10. Quoted in Leonard J. Arrington, *Brigham Young: American Moses* (New York: Alfred A. Knopf, 1985), 409.

11. Young, "Poetry and Sayings," box 6, folder 47.

12. *Time*, Nov. 11, 1957.

Selected Bibliography

Primary Sources

Sea Gull Monument Folder. Archives, Historical Department of the Church of Jesus Christ of Latter-day Saints, Salt Lake City, Utah.

Jack Sears Collection. Mss. 1058, Archives and Manuscripts, Harold B. Lee Library, Brigham Young University, Provo, Utah.

This is the Place Monument Folder. Archives, Historical Department of the Church of Jesus Christ of Latter-day Saints, Salt Lake City, Utah.

This is the Place State Park Folder. Archives, Historical Department of the Church of Jesus Christ of Latter-day Saints, Salt Lake City, Utah.

Mahonri Young Collection. Mss. 4, Archives and Manuscripts, Harold B. Lee Library, Brigham Young University, Provo, Utah.

Secondary Sources

Armstrong et al. *200 Years of American Sculpture*. New York: D. R. Godine, in association with the Whitney Museum of American Art, 1976.

Arrington, Leonard J. *Great Basin Kingdom: Economic History of the Latter-day Saints, 1830-1900*. Lincoln: University of Nebraska Press, 1958.

——————. *Brigham Young: American Moses*. New York: Alfred A. Knopf, 1985.

Art in the United States Capital. Washington, D.C.: U.S. Government Printing Office, 1974.

Avard T. Fairbanks: Eight Decades. A Retrospective Exhibition. Exhibition catalog, Provo, Utah, 1987.

Baker, William J. *Sports in the Western World*. Totowa, NJ: Rowman and Littlefield, 1982.

Beebe, Lucius, and Charles Clegg. *Rio Grande: Mainline of the Rockies*. Berkeley, CA: Howell, 1962.

Biographical Sketches of American Artists. 5th ed. Lansing, MI: State Library, 1924.

Braider, Donald. *George Bellows and the Ashcan School of Painting*. Garden City, NY: Doubleday and Co., 1971.

Broder, Patricia Janis. *Bronzes of the American West*. New York: Harry N. Abrams, 1974.

Brown, Milton W. *American Painting from the Armory Show to the Depression*. Princeton, NJ: Princeton University Press, 1972.

——————. *The Story of the Armory Show*. New York: The Joseph H. Hirshhorn Foundation, [1963].

—————— et al. *American Art: Painting, Sculpture, Architecture, Decorative Arts, Photography*. New York: Harry N. Abrams, 1979.

Conner, Janis and Joel Rosenkranz. *Rediscoveries in American Sculpture: Studio Works, 1893-1939*. Austin: University of Texas Press, 1989.

Cox, Kenyon. *The Classic Point of View*. New York: W. W. Norton Co., 1980.

Craven, Wayne. *American Art: History and Culture*. Madison, WI: Brown and Benchmark, 1994.

Ekdahl, Janis. *American Sculpture: A Guide to Information Sources*. N.p.: Gale Research Co., 1977.

Fairbanks, Eugene F. *A Sculptor's Testimony in Bronze and Stone: The Sacred Sculpture of Avard T. Fairbanks*. Salt Lake City: by the author, n.d.

Fielding, Mantle. *Dictionary of American Painters, Sculptors, and Engravers*. Philadelphia (printed privately for subscribers), 1926.

Francis, Rell G. *Cyrus E. Dallin: Let Justice Be Done*. Springville, UT: Springville Museum of Art, 1976.

Fusco, Peter and H. W. Janson. *The Romantics to Rodin: French Nineteenth-Century Sculpture for North American Collections*. Los Angeles: Los Angeles County Museum of Art, 1980.

Gardner, Albert Ten Eyck. *American Sculpture: A Catalogue of the Collection of the Metropolitan Museum of Art*. Greenwich, CT: distributed by the New York Graphic Society, 1965.

Gibbs, Linda Jones. *Harvesting the Light: The Paris Art Mission and Beginnings of Utah Impressionism*. Salt Lake City: Church of Jesus Christ of Latter-day Saints, 1987.

Goodrich, Lloyd and John I. H. Baur. *American Art of Our Century: Whitney Museum of American Art*. New York: Praeger, 1961.

Haseltine, James L. *100 Years of Utah Painting: Selected Works from the 1840s to the 1940s*. Salt Lake City: Salt Lake Art Center, 1965.

Hinton, Wayne Kendall. "A Biographical History of Mahonri M. Young, a Western American Artist," Ph.D. diss., Brigham Young University, 1974.

Horne, Alice Merrill. *Devotees and Their Shrines: A Handbook of Utah Art*. Salt Lake City: Deseret News Press, 1914.

Jessee, Dean C., comp. *Letters of Brigham Young to His Sons*. Salt Lake City: Deseret Book Co., 1974.

Journal of Discourses. 26 Vols., Liverpool, England, 1874.

Kennedy Galleries are Host to the Hundredth Anniversary Exhibition of Paintings and Sculpture by 100 Artists Associated with The Art Students League of New York. Exhibition catalog, The Art Students League and Kennedy Galleries, New York, 1973.

La Follette, Suzanne. *Art in America*. New York: Harper & Brothers, 1929.

Leek, Thomas. "Ten Formulators of Early Utah Art History." M.A. thesis, Brigham Young University, 1961.

Licht, Fred. *Sculpture: 19th and 20th Centuries*. Greenwich: New York Graphic Society, 1967.

Macomber, Ben. *The Jewel City*. San Francisco: John H. Williams, 1915.

"Mahonri Mackintosh Young—Sculptor and Graver," *Index of Twentieth-Century Artists*. Vol. 2. New York: Research Institute of the College Art Association, 1933-37.

Mather et al. *The Pageant of America: The American Spirit in Art*, Vol. 12. New Haven, CT: Yale University Press, 1927.

Mayer et al. *A Century of American Sculpture: Treasures from Brookgreen Gardens*. New York: Abbeville Press, 1988.

McCausland, Elizabeth. *A. H. Maurer*. New York: Published for the Walker Art Center, A. A. Wyn, Inc., 1951.

Mendelowitz, Daniel M. *A History of American Art*. New York: Holt, Rinehart & Winston, 1970.

Munkittrick, Richard Kendall. *Farming*. New York: Harpers, 1891. (In *Harper's Weekly*, 7 June 1890, supplement, 6 Sept. 1890-17 Jan. 1891.)

Myers, Jerome. *Artist in Manhattan*. New York: American Artists Group, 1930.

Noverr, Douglas A. and Lawrence E. Ziewacy. *Sports in American History, 1865-1980*. Chicago: Nelson-Hall, 1983.

Olpin, Robert S. *Dictionary of Utah Art*. Salt Lake City: Salt Lake Art Center, 1980.

One Hundred Prints by 100 Artists of the Art Students League of New York, 1875-1975. New York: Art Students League of New York, 1975.

Pierce, Patricia Jobe. *The Ten*. Hingham, MA: Pierce Galleries, Inc., 1976.

Pyper, George D. *The Romance of an Old Playhouse*. Salt Lake City: Seagull Press, 1928.

Reed, Henry M. *The A. B. Frost Book*. Rutland, VT: Charles E. Tuttle Co., 1967.

Reed, Walt and Roger Reed. *The Illustrator in America, 1880-1980: A Century of Illustration*. New York: Madison Square Press, Inc., 1984.

Reynolds, Donald Martin. *Masters of American Sculpture: The Figurative Tradition from the American Renaissance to the Millennium*. New York: Abbeville Press, 1993.

Reynolds, George and Janne M. Sjodahl. *Commentary on the Book of Mormon*. 5 vols. Salt Lake City: Deseret Book Co., 1977.

Rheims, Maurice. *19th-Century Sculpture*. New York: Abrams, 1977.

Roberts, Brigham H. *A Comprehensive History of the Church of Jesus Christ of Latter-day Saints*. 6 vols. Provo, UT: Brigham Young University Press, 1965.

Scott, David. *John Sloan*. New York: Watson-Guptill, 1975.

"Sculpture, Drawing, and Etchings by Mahonri Young," Exhibition catalog, *The Sculpture Gallery*. New York, 1918.

Sculpture Drawings and Paintings by Mahonri Young. Exibition catalogue, The Sculptors Gallery, 25 Feb. to 18 Mar. 1918, New York: 1918.

Smith, Joseph Fielding. *Essentials of Church History*. Salt Lake City: Deseret Book Co., 1971.

Smith, Ralph Clifton. *Biographical Index of American Artists*. Baltimore, MD: Williams and Wilkins Co., 1930.

Stegner, Wallace. *The Gathering of Zion: The Story of the Mormon Trail*. Lincoln: University of Nebraska Press, 1981.

Stein, Leo. *Appreciation: Painting, Poetry, and Prose*. New York: Crown, 1947.

Swenson, John A. "The Art Philosophy of Mahonri M. Young." M.A. thesis, Brigham Young University, 1971.

This is the Place: Monument and Mural. Utah State Park and Recreation Commission (text by Allen S. Cornwall). Salt Lake City: Wheelwright Lithographing Co., 1960.

This is the Place Monument Commission. Report to Governor Blood and the Twenty-third Legislature Assembly of Utah, 1939.

Weinhardt, Carl J. *The Most of John Held, Jr*. Brattleboro, VT: The Stephen Greene Press, 1972.

Weitenkampf, Frank. *American Graphic Art*. New York: Macmillan Co., 1924.

Wood, Wilford C. *Joseph Smith Begins His Work*. Salt Lake City: Deseret News Press, 1958.

Yonemori, Shirley Kazuko. "Mahonri Mackintosh Young, Printmaker." M.A. thesis, Brigham Young University, 1963.

Young, Mahonri M. "Sculpture Technique—Modeling Theory," *Encyclopedia Britannica*. 13th ed. Vols. 3, 23, 20. London: Encyclopedia Britannica Co., Ltd., 1926.

——————. "Notes at the Beginning," *Mahonri M. Young: Retrospective Exhibition*. Andover: Phillips Academy, 1940.

Young, Mahonri Sharp. *Brigham Young University and M. Knoedler and Company Inc. Present an exhibition of sculpture, painting, and drawing of Mahonri M. Young from the Brigham Young University art collection.* "Essay by an unidentified son of the artist," 1969.

——————. *The Eight*. New York: Watson-Guptill, 1973.

——————. *Early American Moderns: Painters of the Steiglitz Group*. New York: Watson-Guptill, 1974.

Zigrosser, Carl. *The Artist in America: Twenty-Four Closeups of Contemporary Printmakers*. New York: A. A. Knopf, 1942.

Periodical Literature

Art Digest. "Mahonri Young and His 'Cachet of Life.'" Vol. 8, 15 Mar. 1934, p. 15.

Art News. "Carnegie American Judges Announced." Vol. 26, 15 Sept. 1928, p. 10.

Art News. "Mahonri Young, Paul Dougherty—Macbeth Gallery." Vol. 29, 28 Feb. 1931, p. 12.

Art News. "Pioneer Woman Models Now on Exhibition." Vol. 25, 26 Feb 1927, p. 11.

Arts and Decoration. "American Sculptors Who Have Arrived." Vol. 17, 10 May 1922, p. 20.

Bitton, Davis. "The Ritualization of Mormon History," *Utah Historical Quarterly*, Vol. 43, Winter 1975, pp. 67-85.

Broder, Jane. "The Pioneer Woman, Image in Bronze," *American Art Review*, Vol. 2, 1975, pp. 127-34.

Current Opinion. "Mahonri Young's Artistic Search for the Rhythm of Labor." Vol. 57, Sept. 1914, pp. 200-201.

Dougherty, Paul. *"Rolling His Own*, A New Bronze by Mahonri Young," *Vanity Fair*, Vol. 24, May 1925, p. 59.

Dress and Vanity Fair. "Plastic Interpretations of Labors." Vol. 1, Apr. 1927, p. 182.

DuBois, Guy Pene. "Mahonri Young—Sculptor," *Arts and Decoration*, Vol. 8, Feb. 1918, pp. 169, 188.

Gibbs, Jo. "Mahonri's Drawings," *Art Digest*, Vol. 19, 15 Jan. 1945, p. 20.

Hind, C. Lewis. "Mahonri Young's Drawings," *International Studio*, Vol. 64, Apr. 1918, pp. 103-105.

Hinton, Wayne K. "Mahonri Young and the Church: A View of Mormonism and Art," *Dialogue: A Journal of Mormon Thought*, Vol. 7, Winter 1972, pp. 35-43.

L. G. "Exhibitions in New York," *Arts*, Vol. 15, May 1929, p. 330.

Lewine, J. Lester. "The Bronzes of Mahonri Young," *The International Studio*, Vol. 47, 1912, pp. 76, 79.

Life Magazine. "Mahonri Young's Sculpture Preserves His Mormon Past." Vol. 10, 17 Feb. 1941, pp. 76-79.

Lund, John Farnsworth. "A Visit to the Champ's House," *Utah Historical Quarterly*, Vol. 55, Fall 1987, pp. 335-39.

Lyman, Richard R. "Utah's Famous Sculptor Son," *The Pioneer*, Vol. 20, Mar. 1950, p. 65.

Newsweek. "Mormon Artist." Vol. 16, 23 Sept. 1940, p. 58.

Payne, Frank Owen. "The Tribute of American Sculpture to Labor," *Art and Archeology*, Vol. 6, Aug. 1917, p. 87.

Read, Helen Appleton. "The Pioneer Woman," *Arts*, Vol. 11, Apr. 1927, p. 182.

Rishel, Virginia, ed. "The Rise of Tex Rickard as a Fight Promoter," *Utah Historical Quarterly*, Vol. 55, Fall 1987, pp. 340-48.

Sears, Jack. "Portrait of a Utah Artist, Mahonri Mackintosh Young (1877-1957)," *The Art Bulletin*, Vol. 11, Dec. 1, 1957, p. 39.

Survey. "Town Builders of Today." Vol. 52, 1 July 1924, p. 393.

Time. Vol. 70, 11 Nov. 1957, p. 94.

Touchstone. "An Art Born in the West and Epitomizing the West: Illustrated from the Work of Mahonri Young." Vol. 4, Oct. 1918, pp. 8-18.

Utah Academy of Science, Arts and Letters. "Utah Academy Award to Mahonri Mackintosh Young." Vol. 20, 1945, pp. 21-22.

Watson, Jane. "News and Comment." *Magazine of Art*, Vol. 33, Oct. 1940, pp. 582-84.

Weitenkampf, Frank. "An Etching Sculptor: Mahonri Young." *American Magazine Art*, Vol. 13, Apr. 1924, p. 393.

Wilson, James Patterson. "Art and Artists of the Golden West—A Sculptor and a Painter of Utah." *F.A. Journal*, Vol. 24, Feb. 1911, pp. 96-99.

Young, Mahonri. "Life as Mahonri Sees It." *Touchstone*, Vol. 4, Oct. 1918, pp. 8-16.

Young, Mahonri Sharp. "Mormon Art and Architecture." *Art in America*, May-June, 1970, pp. 66-69.

Zabel, Morton Dauwen. "Chicago's Forty-second Annual Exhibition of American Paintings and Sculpture." *Art and Archaeology*, Vol. 29, Jan. 1930, p. 32.

Index

Pages on which illustrations appear are in **bold** face.